With Hearts, Hands and Voices
Spirituality for Everyday Life

Margot Kässmann
translated from the German by Nathan Lechler
english edition edited by Stephen Brown

Risk
B O O K

WCC Publications, Geneva

Translated from the original German by Nathan Lechler
Mit Herzen, Mund und Händen
Spiritualität im Alltag Leben
Gütersloher Verlagshaus, 2007

Cover design : Marie Arnaud Snakkers

ISBN 978-2-8254-1522-1

No. 118 in the Risk Book Series

Printed in France by IRL

Contents

Foreword to the English Edition

Spirituality has for me always been a key to ecumenical experience. My first encounter with the ecumenical movement was in 1983 at the Sixth Assembly of the World Council of Churches in Vancouver. I was overwhelmed by the worship that took place in a large tent. Celebrating with more than 4,000 people from different cultures and nations was at times disturbing but mostly encouraged my faith. I realized that the liturgy of my own church was only one example of the many ways in which we can praise God. And I thus enriched my faith.

Many Christians have had similar experiences at large WCC gatherings, as well as at regional and local meetings on a much smaller scale. Keeping silence with one another, meditating, listening to music or being confronted with art – a spiritual approach to our faith cuts across the borders of confession, culture and language. Spirituality is nourished by the sources of our fathers and mothers in faith, and at the same time cannot be imprisoned by boundaries of tradition because it develops new forms and dynamics along the way. We are now experiencing that in my own church in connection with pilgrimages. In 2005 we reopened a Cistercian pathway following the route taken by monks who left their monastery in 1163 to found a new community. Many people are now following that route for a day or even for the whole 330 kilometres. Parishes along the route are beginning to offer hospitality to the pilgrims, while on the Internet new routes and ideas are added to the first initiative, and new pilgrim paths to other monasteries in our church are being started. There is indeed a great need for opportunities to experience our faith with body and soul.

The spiritual ecumenical experience is also lived out in the daily worship of our church. Today, in the hymn book of my Lutheran church, one can find a Hallelujah-Praise from the Pacific as well as a Kyrie from the Orthodox tradition. Thus, in our worship, we experience that we are part of a family of brothers and sisters worldwide who are inspired and led by the gospel in praising God. Yes, indeed, we can learn from one another on our spiritual journey.

At a time when the ecumenical situation often seems tense and not really encouraging, it can be helpful to concentrate on our common experience of faith. We share the one Bible, the Apostles' Creed, the Lord's Prayer. Whenever I pray with brothers and sisters I experience a great strength in this communion that cuts across all borders of nation and confession. I hope that the ecumenical movement is able to find new courage in this experience. This is especially necessary when we are challenged and confronted by other faiths and by secularization. The ecumenical movement was started by missionaries who found that it was difficult to preach the gospel when the differences between the confessions were so great. In a few years we will be remembering the great World Mission Conference at Edinburgh in 1910 that was the spark for the ecumenical movement. I am quite certain that we face similar challenges today.

This Risk Book is a translation of a German edition published in early 2007. While it exemplifies a specifically Lutheran approach to spirituality, I am sure it has an ecumenical dimension because Christians have spirituality in common, as a common search for an experience of faith. Or as I said in the foreword to the German edition: spirituality is an ecumenical opportunity. Thus I am grateful to the WCC for its initiative to translate the book into English. I hope it will contribute to a fruitful discussion about ecumenical worship and spirituality, and encourage many people to find their own spiritual way of living the Christian faith in daily life.

Foreword: The Treasure Chest of Christian Spirituality

God is no longer taboo. Sometimes, when I'm talking to people I thought were completely secular in outlook, I'm amazed by how interested they are in matters of faith. For example, I was once explaining to a journalist my belief in meditation as one way towards God, when she told me that she'd been practising yoga for years and that she, too, was certain there was something divine in it; but she'd always felt the church was so dry, so constricting – and yet, she couldn't help wondering …

They make me sad, all these missed opportunities. Here in front of me was a young woman interested in faith, but unable to find a home in our church. And yet we have such a wealth of spiritual tradition! It seems to me like a treasure chest, and all we have to do is open it up. If we did that, we could pick out the precious items it contains – some of them we would put back, some we would polish up and use, and some we might even dare to rework, to help them better fit our lives today.

What I want to do with this small book is to encourage us to open up that treasure chest and wipe the dust off here and there, but also to start exploring it, amazed and over-joyed at the gems it contains. I am convinced that there is no need to roam distant lands and comb foreign cultures to find new ways to approach God. There are many courses about silence and meditation, pilgrimage and stillness, but my concern is to strengthen the appeal of Christian spiritu-ality, explain the foundations on which it stands, shed light on the tensions within it and, most of all, reveal the pos-sibilities it offers.

Surveys tell us that more and more people are asking religious questions and seeking security in faith and prayer. The greatest need that we see today, however, is for a living experience of religion, a tangible faith. Here there seems to me to be one vital question: is our church in a position to offer a specifically Christian experience, or do we see the experiential dimension as something that cannot be inte-grated into church life? For it seems, at least, that many people do not expect to find the answers to their spiritual search in the church.

At the same time, though, there is great demand for opportunities offered by the church such as pilgrimages, meditation, and monastic and silent retreats. There was massive interest in the 'spirituality hall' at the 2005 Hanover Kirchentag, a Protestant festival that brings together thousands of people every two years. Indeed, more books were sold at that venue than anywhere else at the event.

Today, huge value is placed on spirituality, not least as *the* great opportunity of the future for the church. And yet for all the talk, nobody seems to know quite what 'spirituality' actually is. It's virtually impossible to define it in a few words.[1] It brings together 'faith, devotional practice and ways to shape one's life' and 'therefore offers an alternative to late-Protestant religiosity, which can become focused solely on words, or on actions or on feelings'.[2] German theologian Fulbert Steffensky attempts to define the concept of spirituality as a 'well-formed attentiveness' or an 'experience of the oneness of life'.[3]

The New Testament repeatedly talks about God's Spirit. The Greek word used for this is *pneuma*, which was translated into Latin as *spiritus*. So, in John's Gospel, Jesus says, 'God is spirit, and his worshippers must worship in spirit and truth' (John 4:24). Thus, 'spirit' stands for the dimension of faith that goes beyond our world of time and space, for that which is within, for God's presence, which is our continual inspiration. Spirituality is also the dimension of faith that is opened up to us by the third person of the Trinity, the Holy Spirit. It is God's Spirit who makes our relationship to God tangible – a relationship centred on Jesus Christ and filled with strength by the Spirit.

However, there are also some critical questions that might well be asked of today's new enthusiasm for spirituality.

---

[1] Various ideas are contained in the *Evangelischer Erwachsenenkatechismus* (Protestant Catechism for Adults), Gütersloher Verlagshaus, Gütersloh, 2000 (6th edn), pp. 739ff.

[2] *Evangelische Spiritualität* (Protestant Spirituality), Gütersloher Verlagshaus, Gütersloh, 1979, pp. 10ff.

[3] Fulbert Steffensky, *Schwarzbrotspiritualität* (Rye-bread Spirituality), Radius, Stuttgart, 2005, pp. 17ff.

Is it not a bit Catholic or pre-Reformation? Is spirituality just a buzzword that can distract Protestants from social engagement? Ought Protestants really to be meditating? Hasn't it got something to do with the occult? What about the intellect and the Enlightenment? Isn't it going to lead Catholics back towards mysticism? Aren't things like Latin chants going to mean a retreat to the days before the Second Vatican Council? How are we to fit the Orthodox veneration of icons into a post-Enlightenment theology? And do we not need clear boundaries – to distinguish us from Zen Buddhism, for instance? Is it possible to integrate yoga into Christianity? Should sensory experience be playing this kind of role in Christian faith?

A while ago, I led a service in the stunning Church of St Michael in Hildesheim in northern Germany. The church, which is nearly a thousand years old, has been declared a World Heritage Site. While I was there, I kept looking up at the arches in the transept. These are very simple, but they carry a striking pattern of red and white stripes. The load-bearing element is a series of tall, noble pillars. On top of each of these stand two smaller pillars. Atop each of those are another two, and at the very top, just below the vault, the pattern is completed by a positively playful addition of another set of little pillars. To me, this seems a good image for the spiritual opportunities that we have. When the fundamental, load-bearing pillars are in place, the structure can withstand tension and diversity.

The first part of this book, then, which is symbolized by the grand, load-bearing pillars of St Michael's Church in Hildesheim, explains the four fundamentals of Christian spirituality which I believe must be made clear if we are to avoid confusion and even, sometimes, to set the limits that are necessary. In the second part, I want to present the tensions that are, it seems to me, always inherent in spirituality. Spirituality is not some nicely packaged concept, quick to learn and easy to use. At the same time, it is not a question of turning away from the world or retreating from it. I will use dialogues with historical and fictional characters to shed light on these tensions. This second part is represented by the smaller pillars in St Michael's Church constructed on top of the larger ones. Lastly, the third part will explore the freedom and the joyful diversity of the spiritual opportunities that we have, reflected in the little pillars that rise up to the vault of St Michael's Church. This is the time to be open, to take risks, to be creative and to experiment, in order for each of us to find out where we can put down our spiritual roots.

This book does not try to contribute to any academic discussion of the issue of spirituality. These days, there is no end of literature about the subject.[4] Of course, I aim to deal with the subject clearly, but also to describe the various approaches in an appealing way as I show the opportunities afforded by spirituality. I want to encourage people to find their own spiritual way, as well as to spark discussions within congregations and parishes about how we can go about offering spirituality to people at a local level in this age of spiritual questioning. The book also addresses certain fashionable ideas about spirituality whereby people believe that anything can be given a Christian label, and which have led to the rise of a kind of spiritual supermarket. Nevertheless, my main aim is to encourage involvement with the experiential side of faith – becoming aware of it through the senses rather than being fixated by words, and by loving life and welcoming experience instead of imprisoning ourselves in narrowness and strictness.

In studying the ancient texts, I've noticed that stepping way from exclusively intellectual approaches and allowing the emotions to become a part of the life of faith apparently comes more easily to women than to men. Many men react to emotional approaches to faith by quickly becoming defensive and retreating to the supposedly safer shores of familiar statements of faith, orders of service or formulations. Clearly, if we are to find a balance, we must incorporate both masculine and feminine characteristics into our church, for,

---

[4] See, for instance, Peter Zimmerling, *Evangelische Spiritualität* (Protestant Spirituality), Taschenbuch, Göttingen, 2003; Manfred Josuttis, *Heiligung des Lebens* (The Sanctification of Life), Gütersloher Verlagshaus, Gütersloh, 2004.

as I see it, it is vital on the one hand that we keep a balance between faith and reason, and on the other that we welcome the feelings, the senses and the inner awareness of God. Equality between men and women has been an issue in the church for years, and our common search for a lived spirituality may well have an important contribution to make in this area, too.

One more thing: the reflections in this book come from a Protestant – and specifically Lutheran – perspective. This finds its expression particularly in the focus on the Bible and the tradition of hymns and song. Nevertheless, I am convinced that spirituality is a central factor for ecumenism. Indeed, 'the ecumenical movement itself has been understood by its supporters as a spiritual experience'.[5] My desire is to grasp the ecumenical opportunity that spirituality affords us. Christianity in Western Europe often seems desiccated and lacking in joy and appears to hold little relevance to everyday life. Precious little is seen of the good news of the faith that sets us free. And yet we have such a wonderful spiritual tradition! I do not believe there is any need to go searching for far-Eastern rituals to help us experience Christian spirituality when we can draw from our own wells. But we must learn to know our roots in order to experience diversity; as we travel, confessional differences will doubtless come to light. Still, this area of spirituality is one where we can learn from each other, discover the old treasures we have in common and find new ones together.

When two people go on pilgrimage together, they will have spiritual experiences that do not fit, as it were, into either of their denominational boxes. As foreign as the Orthodox use of icons in spirituality may be to me, icons can also enrich Protestantism. As annoying as many Orthodox theologians may find women's spiritual impulses in theology, they also acknowledge connections within those impulses to their own reflections on the Holy Spirit. As strange as the Catholic veneration of saints may be to Protestants, it can remind

---

[5] Hans-Martin Barth, *Spiritualität* (Spirituality), Vandenhoeck and Ruprecht, Göttingen, 1993, p. 8.

us how fundamental the remembrance and recollection of our own fathers and mothers in the faith can be for our own walk with God. As irritating as the more Charismatic elements of the Pentecostal churches can be, we can see there the emotional abandon of worshipping Christ that has been lost in some other traditions. In short, in spirituality, we can all learn from each other and grow with each other.

In a day when some warn that the ecumenical movement is becoming stagnant, I nevertheless see intentional fellowship between men and women of different Christian traditions – on pilgrims' paths, at meditation centres, in choirs. Perhaps one day, alongside the 'movement for life and work', which seeks to create church unity through common action, and the 'movement for faith and order', which seeks unity through doctrinal convergence, there will be a genuine 'movement for experiential spirituality' that will provide new impetus for the ecumenical movement.

In all of this, I think it important that we approach spirituality with a certain lightness of heart. In some of its forms, spirituality runs the risk of sinking into legalism, if pressure arises to keep the seven weeks of Lent, for instance, or if one is obliged to perform certain practices at specific times. Of course, the practice of spirituality requires a certain discipline and regularity, but its most important aspects are the joy of faith and the love of God. I'm often cheered by Martin Luther's saying that preaching cannot be done without humour. This inner freedom that allows us to look at ourselves with amusement definitely has a place in spirituality. There is a poem by Hanns Dieter Hüsch that I think wonderfully expresses this tension between seriousness and cheerfulness:

Summer Psalm

Incidentally, O Lord,
I wonder whether you might send us
a great big summer.
Send all the families a big basket of peace
and lots of hope-giving views of green and blue.
Meadows and streams and pristine beaches.
Months of quiet.

Remove the scream from this world
and command stillness.
And Lord, that means that those who make war
must lose their jobs.
And those who have no jobs
must lose their hopelessness.
And the mighty must not become mafia.
We all have a role to play and work to do
in making life run more slowly
and the world turn less frenetically
that men may look at each other a little longer
and say: we love you!
O Lord, bless us with this quiet.
May this quiet blow into the ears of all those
who make our days so fast
and yet, at the same time, so short, so breathless.
O Lord our God, we beg you: do this!
That our hearts may once again catch their breath,
our eyes cease to roam
and our ears hear aright
and stop forgetting everything.
And Lord, those who would steal our peace –
send them a lightning bolt up the backside,
that they might recognize the inhumanity of their actions
and leave human beings on whom your favour rests
in peace.
And once again, Lord, we ask
that you would bless this suggestion of ours all over the world.
Because that's how it should be, now and forever!
Thanks. Amen.

Four Foundational Pillars

'Is that really Christian? Should it be allowed in church?'

When I hear questions like these, I always think that if the cornerstone is fixed, then many things are possible! The Apostle Paul himself had to tackle the question of where to draw boundaries, and, as I understand it, he highlighted two principles. The first was to make sure that whatever was at issue had Jesus Christ as its focus and not some other person or thing. Sometimes, during the design process for a logo or symbol for some church institution, I end up saying, 'But we've already got one – the cross!' The cross is known all over the world and is instantly identifiable as a Christian symbol. It is our centre, our focus, our distinctive identity. It stands for suffering and death, for the forgiveness of sins and freedom, for victory over death and for resurrection, and it is the hallmark of Christian belief around the world. In the cross, we see what is Christian and what is not.

Paul's second principle is: is this about building up the community of the church or does it have some other aim? Christianity is a religion of community. While it is true that we believe as individuals and that each of us has our own relationship to God, we do these things *with each other* from start to finish. This can sometimes be demanding and can doubtless mean being in conflict with each other – that much is clear from Paul's first letter to the Corinthians in the Bible. Yet our religion must always be lived with an awareness of our brothers and sisters in the faith. To be an egotist and yet live the Christian life is a contradiction in terms.

However, once he was sure that the heart of something was Jesus Christ and the well-being of the community, Paul was able to be very generous. In the face of demands for strict laws and clear-cut regulations, he argued for an openness of heart. Being a Jew to the Jews and a Greek to the Greeks is not a matter of squeezing oneself to fit the spirit of the age – it's a matter of inner freedom. It means acceptance instead of narrow-mindedness, being open to the new rather than clinging to the familiar. If the foundations are in place, a lot can be thought and a lot can be done.

Where there is charity and wisdom
there is neither fear nor ignorance.
Where there is patience and humility
There is neither anger nor disturbance.
Where there is poverty with joy,
there is neither covetousness nor avarice.
Where there is inner peace and meditation,
there is neither anxiousness nor dissipation.
Where there is fear of the Lord to guard the house,
there the enemy cannot gain entry.
Where there is mercy and discernment,
there is neither excess nor hardness of heart.
Francis of Assisi[6]

The Bible

Many times, I've been asked the famous question, 'If you could take one book with you on a desert island, what would it be?' Sometimes I'm almost embarrassed to give my reply: the Bible. I'm a bishop, after all; it sounds as though my training has conditioned me to give the right answer. But, in fact, I am simply convinced, as a human being and as a Christian, that you can never finish reading this Book of Books. For one thing, I am constantly encountering passages that surprise me anew, and thinking, 'I've never seen that in there before!' For instance, I only discovered the two midwives of Pharaoh's day, Shiphrah and Puah, when I was preparing for the World Day of Prayer. Only by chance did I discover that Joseph and his eleven brothers also had a sister, called Dinah. For a long time, I overlooked the short verses about Pilate's wife. I'm always surprised about the differing emphases of the four gospel writers. And the first time I tracked Paul's journeys carefully through the accounts in his letters was for a lecture – and in doing so, I realized Paul was, in a manner of speaking, the first pioneer of globalization!

There is another reason why you can never finish reading the Bible, and that is that a biblical text does not carry

---

[6] Francis of Assisi, *Francis and Clare: The Complete Works*, trans. R. J. Armstrong and I. C. Brady, Paulist Press, New York/Malwah, NJ, 1982, p. 35.

one and the same meaning for the whole of life, and holds different meanings for different people depending on their circumstances. For example, there's an extraordinary diversity in the way many people experience Psalm 23. For many, these words provide comfort and encouragement in many different circumstances. However, there are others who feel an inner resistance when they hear the words 'your rod and your staff, they comfort me'. For them, this awakens associations of beatings from childhood that were supposed to 'do them good'. It was a long time before I realized that this verse could have associations of that kind.

As far as I am concerned, I have noticed that biblical texts continually speak anew into new contexts and situations. It's more than 25 years since I preached my first sermon. The lectionaries of scripture readings used in worship mean that every few years pastors will find the same suggested text for their sermons. During that time, however, things have changed – the pastor may even have a different parish – and the context within which the pastor is preaching is inevitably different. In addition, those who preach and those who listen are influenced by events such as the attacks of 11 September 2001, the 2004 tsunami and the 2006 soccer World Cup.

You can never finish reading the Bible

The text of the Bible is a record of an experience of faith, which enters into dialogue with believers in their own context and situation. That's why it can never be fully read, never finished – because it is always part of a dialogue. Reading the Bible is the meeting point between the recorded work of God and the experienced reality of God. In this three-way relationship between God, reader and context, the passages of the Bible are reflected anew and made relevant again. You really can never come to the end of reading the Bible.

For me, it's a real tragedy that so many people in my homeland of Germany have hardly any knowledge of the Bible anymore. In my country, it was Martin Luther who made the first translation of the Bible into the language of the people. He wanted people to be able to read it for themselves. He founded schools for boys and even for girls, setting in motion a process of education on an unprecedented scale.

Faith is a gift

The film *Luther*, which opened in German cinemas in 2003 on the eve of Reformation Day, depicts this brilliantly. Joseph Fiennes, playing the title role, bears little resemblance to the portrait of Luther by Cranach that most of us know – he's too slim, for one thing – but the film shows very clearly how Luther did not rely on others or appeal to tradition, but read for himself, searched for understanding for himself, and fought for truth and insight. When in his theological understanding he came to realize that nothing and nobody could come between him and Christ – no doctrine, no priest, no tradition and not even a pope – it was a liberation. He gave himself completely to this truth: that faith is a gift from God to people, and that people can therefore live fully in God's grace and free from fear. Luther did not shy away from this, but courageously took up responsibility in the world as a consequence of his faith. We could use more of that today!

The Bible is of central importance to Protestants, in particular, in offering guidance. Indeed, the whole Reformation is, in the final analysis, a development of Luther's study of the Bible. The film *Luther* shows this beautifully, when Luther's fatherly teacher, Staupitz (played by Bruno Ganz), wants to send him to study in Wittenberg. 'Have you ever read the Bible?' he asks. The young Luther, then a monk, answers, 'The gospels? No.' In that exchange is an indication of the immense change that is about to take place. A number of years later and sequestered in Wartburg Castle, Luther translated the Bible. In the film, he gives his translation to Frederick III (played brilliantly by Peter Ustinov). This is historically inaccurate: in reality, the reformer and the Elector never met. Nevertheless, the scene shows the nature of the gift and the huge challenge represented to the power of the church in that age by giving people the chance to read for themselves.

The translation of the Bible into German was a revolutionary event. And yet today many people are completely unaware of this.

The responsibility of faith

Again and again, people tell me that Christianity's not interesting, and then when I ask what they've read in the Bible that's so terrible or what their difficulties really are, the real answer often comes to the surface: they've never even dipped into the Bible for themselves. This is tragic! The complete Bible has now been translated into 392 languages, while the New Testament is available in 1,012. There are some people in the world to whom it means a great deal when they are finally able to read the scriptures in their own language.

Christians all over the world hold the Bible first and foremost as the foundational book of our faith, the fundamental pillar, the central point of reference. At international church conferences I'm often amazed how, on some issues, this helps us to understand each other. Everybody is familiar with the Book of Jonah; we all know what is meant by 'the Beatitudes'; and everyone has heard of Gethsemane. This all goes to show that the Bible is a key to understanding across cultural and national borders. It is the witness and source of our faith.

The Bible has also left its mark on our culture, in literature, music and theatre. If we do not know the Bible we cannot understand European history and architecture. For the Bible is also our cultural heritage, and only those who read it for themselves can understand what it means and can dispute or affirm the claims it makes.

The Bible has marked our culture

In this respect, the so-called historical-critical method of biblical interpretation seems to me to be of great help, and not the deterrence that some think it is. Historical-critical interpretation allows me to find out the context and the age in which a book of the Bible appeared, whether it was written by one person or compiled by many, and whether any parts of it are later insertions. And there's no need to be a student of theology to find this information. There are up-to-date and easily understood reference works that explain unfamiliar concepts and help us to classify the various books and authors of the Bible and hence better to understand the Bible as a whole.

Reading the Bible does not require learning Greek, Hebrew and Latin; that's the great achievement of the translations of Martin Luther and the other translations that exist. But the reader should remember that these *are* translations. My desire is that we in our age seek guidance from the Bible, and also that we once again find a way to speak as Christians in Europe. We must speak of what is important for us – of faith in Jesus Christ, of the fact that God created the world, that the earth belongs to God and we are its stewards, charged with cultivating it and protecting it responsibly. Many Christians seem to have been struck dumb on these issues. People will talk about everything and everyone except their own faith. Here lies a great challenge: how do we find a language of our own that will express the relationship between our faith and reason without simply falling into the stereotypical formulations that one finds, for instance, in US culture?

In this individualistic society, it comes down to saying what *I* believe, what *I* am convinced of and what sustains *me*. People today will be persuaded by the resources of the Bible coupled with personal faith. In the *Letters and Papers from Prison* of Dietrich Bonhoeffer, the 100th anniversary of whose birth we commemorated in February 2006, we can find this remark:

> It is not for us to prophesy the day … when men will once more be called so to utter the word of God that the world will be changed and renewed by it. It will be a new language, perhaps quite non-religious, but liberating and redeeming – as was Jesus' language; … it will be the language of a new righteousness and truth, proclaiming God's peace with men and the coming of his kingdom.[7]

[7] Dietrich Bonhoeffer, *Letters and Papers from Prison: The Enlarged Edition*, 3rd edn, ed. E. Bethge, trans. R. Fuller et al., SCM Press, London, 1971, p. 300.

And that's what we need to do as a church and as Christians if we are to help people understand that *they can rely on God*, that God can be the solid ground in their life – like a rock, so to speak; Jesus can mean something to them in a truly personal way. How can we find words to say this that are not sentimental, nor old-fashioned, nor pushy, but just persuasive? Whenever I hear the criticism that the church shouldn't pander to the media, that Christian truth can't be packaged into 90-second soundbites, I find myself thinking that any of Jesus' parables could probably be spoken within a minute and a half. That is to say, Jesus could powerfully express the truths of the faith in simple words and with everyday examples. And people can still understand those parables even after 2,000 years have passed. The Good Samaritan, the Prodigal Son, the mustard seed as a picture of the kingdom of heaven – none of it is complicated, but it is all charged with spiritual meaning. So language, too, has spiritual significance.

Poetry is probably the most beautiful language of faith. The poetic passages in the Bible, from the Psalms to the 'hymn of love' in 1 Corinthians 13, have always especially moved people's hearts. Even today, when we so often grow weary of just too many words, poetry can reach our hearts and touch our souls. So let's discover the Bible anew, and find within it the language of faith in poetry.

Suggestion

Take a Bible in your hand and resolve to read one book from within it – a passage every day. Begin, if you can, with one of the four gospels. Mark is the shortest and oldest; Luke is an excellent storyteller; Matthew contains the Sermon on the Mount. Decide on one of these three. John has quite a different style, which you'll be able to notice better if you have first read one of the others.

Find a set time to read – maybe a passage every evening, or half an hour every Sunday. A set time and a set rhythm are helpful.

You may be able to find a family member or a friend who's also interested. When two people read and talk about the same reading, they can both get much more from the content.

8

> After a gospel, read Genesis, which contains the great foundational stories of the Old Testament – Creation, the Flood, the Tower of Babel – leading into the stories of Abraham, Isaac and Jacob and ending with the story of Joseph.
>
> If you don't want to choose a book yourself, you can follow a Bible-reading plan. This takes you through selected biblical books throughout the year. Or you can follow a guide such as the 'Watchwords' produced by the Moravian Church and available on the Internet (www.moravian.org.uk). It selects a verse from the Old Testament and a passage from the New Testament for every day over one year, and helps many people to step into each new morning with a verse from the scriptures. This, too, can be a good way of becoming more familiar with that supporting pillar of our faith, the Bible.

Worship

One often hears complaints about Lutheran worship: it is without emotion, without love, it has no appeal. A recent survey of young people coming up for confirmation noted:

> Almost all find [the service] 'boring'; they see the ritual as 'slow', 'formal' and 'too serious', with 'old-fashioned music'; they find the preaching difficult or impossible to follow and feel absolutely no sense of 'community'.[8]

There's no doubt in my mind that we simply cannot afford our church services to be without love! Each person who comes into one of our services must go out again newly empowered to face everyday life. This can happen in a 'normal' service, or it can happen through one of the new forms of services, with newer music or a changed format, or in family services or services that use gospel music. A church service should strengthen people in faith, enfold them in community, stimulate them to think and help them to sing God's praise and bring their thanks to God. In this

---

[8] *Evangelischer Erwachsenenkatechismus*, p. 319 (English translation prepared for this publication).

respect, each parish needs to think for itself how to bring more life into its services, so that everyone taking part can find spiritual strength and experience community.

On the other hand, I object to the attitude that suggests we can reduce communal worship to a means of meeting our own personal spiritual needs. A service of worship is also a place where we offer our service to God. A consumerist attitude, however, that has become very popular says that worship ought to do something for me. But, as the hymn 'All people that on earth do dwell' puts it, we are to 'enter the gates with praise', and that's true as well. In that sense, worship is not for my benefit; it is simply about praising my Creator. 'A service of worship is a celebration in which the community is visited by someone else – by God, who desires to share with the community through his word and invite it to his table. God's call awakens people's answer. A service of worship is therefore both God's service to us and our service before God.'[9] We would do well to understand this anew.

Psalm 147 says, 'How good it is to sing praises to our God!' That means that it brings God joy when I sing his praise, when we pray to him together, when we hear his word. Worship is a dialogue between God and his people. We hear and answer; we ask for and experience his presence. What the liturgy does is to give structure to this celebration and provide it with a form – as indeed all celebrations have certain rituals and forms that are repeated, alongside the constant exploration of new things. Thomas Kabel writes:

> The peel of bells calls us to a spiritual adventure. The journey begins as soon as the service is opened – a journey from everyday existence into spiritual life. The person leading the liturgy guides us through the obstacles and hurdles on our path to the essence of our true nature.[10]

We need to rediscover this basic insight.

---

[9] Ibid., p. 516 (English translation prepared for this publication).

[10] Thomas Kabel, *Handbuch Liturgische Präsenz. Zur praktischen Inszenierung des Gottesdienstes* (Liturgical Handbook: Towards the Practical Staging of the Worship Service), vol. 1, Gütersloher Verlagshaus, Gütersloh, 2002, p. 25 (English translation prepared for this publication).

It may also help us to gain a greater understanding of the worth of communal worship if we begin to understand that we are coming to the house of God to praise our God and celebrate our faith together. And it should be a celebration! We can celebrate quietly, in smaller groups, or we can celebrate with great noise as a great multitude. And our celebration always draws us into community – including through the stories of our fathers and mothers in the faith passed on to us through words and music, through liturgy and the church building itself.

In his book *Schwarzbrotspiritualität* (Rye-bread Spirituality), Fulbert Steffensky passionately argues against explaining in detail every single thing that happens in a service. He argues that the old rituals and forms have a language of their own that we can enter into without needing to understand everything. He also holds that Protestants should not constantly overestimate the significance of the sermon:

> We are, perhaps, a little obsessed with the idea that people can understand and accept only that which is expressly brought to their conscious attention. Conscious understanding is not the only form of understanding. Talking is for those who do not respect form, ritual and gesture. [11]

There is also deep significance to be found in keeping the old forms of worship. There are, of course, new forms of worship and these may be easier to understand and more relevant to people today – gospel music services, for instance. And readers can indeed learn not simply to reel off the biblical texts but to read them with expression – even with different people reading the parts of different characters.

Old and new forms

The choice of hymns can be made with the congregation's singing in mind, and new or less well known hymns can be practised before the service begins. I believe there is a place for applause in church, if a congregation spontaneously

---

[11] Steffensky, *Schwarzbrotspiritualität*, p. 87 (English translation prepared for this publication).

wants to express its affirmation of something. But something is lost when we make everything so easy to digest: a Gloria is a Gloria and a Kyrie is a Kyrie. There ought also to be an explanation of when to stand, when to sit and when – if one can – to kneel. There is an old rule of thumb: sit to listen, stand to sing and kneel to pray. Congregations can make their own decisions about this, and give notice of what is expected so as to avoid the confusion I have often seen where people spend the first half of the Lord's Prayer timidly standing up one after the other, because some people think that's what one is supposed to do and the others then start to think, 'Well, I don't want to be the only one sitting down.'

Nevertheless, while explaining everything might soften the stiffness sometimes felt in church services, it can also sometimes lead to a service degenerating into chat. It can create a nice atmosphere, yes, but it might as well be an afternoon spent in a neighbour's garden. Liturgy means a set of forms for worship that can be relied upon, with certain recognizable rituals, gestures and customs. In *Schwarzbrotspiritualität* (p. 73 and onwards), Fulbert Steffensky describes how space and ritual create a feeling of being at home. This means that I don't need to understand everything down to the last detail, but can entrust myself to the ritual and enter into it. I don't *need* to spend every church service wondering if I assent to every phrase in the Apostles' Creed word for word; rather, I can give myself to this tradition that has been shared by Christians across the world since AD 325. I can join in singing hymns that I might find jarring but with which I am part of a community that exists throughout time.

Moreover, Christian community is always an experience of community in the here and now, but one that spans the globe and transcends past and future. We can't switch it about every week, showing video clips each Sunday or turning church into a talk show. This can devalue worship, which has to be more than short-term entertainment.

We need to worship God in our churches as a community: while the Christian faith places a great deal of importance on individuals' own relationships to God, it always sees them as part of a community. We pray to God on our own, but we join together to hear God's word to us, to sing together and to pray. Part of Christian spirituality lies in having a community of people with whom one listens, sings and prays. We should not take this freedom for granted. The earliest Christians risked their lives to meet together; indeed, even today, believers in places such as China and Indonesia risk their lives simply by taking part in church worship.

I am all too aware that, for many people, this sense of community is no longer a reality. In 2006, the Council of the Evangelical Church in Germany published a discussion paper entitled *Church of Freedom*, which set out targets to be reached by the year 2030. These targets included raising the percentage of church members attending services from 4 per cent to 10 per cent. This seems to me to be a major challenge. The plan to achieve this increase involves setting up special congregations, such as youth churches, and gospel music churches, targeted at specific groups. It may of course be a good idea to concentrate on specific areas or groups, but a local community that spans different social groups can create greater stability and a sense of belonging. This is something I see time and again in country parishes, where business people and single mothers sit side by side on the church council, while teachers and farmers take part in the same service. We should not underestimate this kind of community, which is not created by like-minded people seeking each other out, but arises from shared faith in a shared place.

This community is not just a local but also a worldwide phenomenon. When we are baptized, it is into communion with God and all other Christians. It means the acceptance of a child into the family of God. Baptism is not merely a family event. It is a public sign and rite of community. As Lutherans, we understand baptism as being one of the two sacraments, alongside the Lord's Supper. Together, they are essential to our worship and spirituality.

That's why it should take place as part of public worship, rather than be a quiet little affair that nobody knows about. A celebration of baptism is an experience of spirituality: we call on the Spirit of God and stand before God and each other. Particularly now, when families are becoming smaller, the family of God is an important point of reference. A church wedding, too, should be seen not as a stage-managed event but as the moment where a couple comes before God and before this same community to say their 'yes' to each other. The church community also provides a context for people to stand together at times of crisis. The same is true for rites of passage such as services for those starting school and other church ceremonies such as confirmation services, wedding anniversaries and services for commemoration of baptism.

The hallmark of community

Probably the greatest experience of the meaning of this community lies in the Lord's Supper. Jesus made what one might call a hallmark out of eating together. He would sit down to eat with people whom the rest of society had cast aside. Even his Last Supper he shared with the one who would betray him. When we gather round that table today, we too are part of a community, the *communio sanctorum* – the communion of saints. This means communion with God, with the Risen One, but also with the *communio sanctorum* – the community of women and men through the ages who have trusted God, both those who have gone before us and those who come after us, Christians of all traditions and nations all around the world. During the Lord's Supper, I am often quite moved when I remember that we all stand united before God, even if we celebrate his Supper in divided churches.

All around the world

Worship means liturgy, the experience of community, and the tradition in which I find myself. The Lord's Supper is the key to Christian spirituality, I believe. And this is why so many people feel the pain of not being able to celebrate it together with all other Christians in the world.

I do want to see changes in the way we hold our church services: it ought to be a joy to come together to worship God! All too often, though, the people who say that things need to change are the ones who hardly ever go to church themselves. They don't even take the trouble to get to know the liturgy – so changing the times of services, for example, is going to have very little effect on how much they take part. But worship only comes to life if we share the experience of it with each other. As a bishop, I enjoy the luxury that the services I take part in are well attended, very carefully prepared affairs, but I'm well aware that these special services are not the norm. We need, therefore, to use new methods to strengthen the experience of community in normal worship.

In the past, the church service was *the* main event. There were no distractions, no television, no cinema. If you wanted to see other people and hear the latest gossip, you went to church, as it was the only community event there was. It was the one place where people could go to meet each other and exchange news and views. We cannot recreate that today. Nor can we spend all our time putting on big, staged 'events'. What we can do as Christians is simply to make a point of seeking out this community regularly. Pastors, church councillors, lay-readers and preachers should prepare services with love and care. But you cannot measure the success of a service simply by the numbers of people attending or with a consumer mentality that asks, 'Does it do anything for me?' I'm all in favour of efforts to increase the numbers of people taking part in our services, but not at the expense of dumbing down or diluting their content. No, what we need to do is to let people know that they are invited to worship God in the joy of his presence, in the beauty of the church building, of love for his word and of the sense of community.

There are, of course, always ways one can suggest improvements and become involved. In the United States I went to a service where, at the start, all who were there for the first time were invited to stand and introduce themselves, and received a special greeting. There was nothing forced about it; it simply facilitated community. I was once in a church in Brazil where they began by announcing who had donated this week's flowers, giving it a personal touch. Congregations need to preserve their heritage, but should also be open to new things. If people have criticisms to make, they can be invited to share them constructively – because, as everyone involved knows, a balance needs to be struck between tradition and innovation.

Our spirituality as individual Christians can take shape in a way quite unique to us, using the many possibilities that our faith affords us. Nevertheless, it is vital to make sure that it is grounded in the spirituality of our tradition and community.

Suggestion

Go and attend a 'normal' Sunday service. Is there anything you recognize from other services you've been to? What helps you? What bothers you? You might want to plan a regular visit to a service – say, once a month: worshipping together is another part of spirituality that needs practice. The first time you go into a service, there's a lot that's bound to feel strange. It's perfectly normal. It takes time to feel at home with the liturgy. Often, there is an order of service. In my tradition this will include a Psalm, through a Kyrie, a Gloria, some prayer and Bible passage to the sermon, and from there to intercession, the Lord's Prayer and the blessing.

Is there a church in which you could make yourself at home? One possibility is to attend the church in your own neighbourhood, where you'll meet the people you see in everyday life. On the other hand, your decision might be swayed by a particular building, a preacher, the music or simply the times of the services. And, once you've been there a few times, if you have suggestions on how things could be changed, people will be glad to listen to them, discuss them and maybe even act on them. One other thing: speaking as a preacher, I find most constructive feedback on my sermons helpful and positive. I think that's true of most people who preach, as we do invest a lot of time in preparation.

Prayer

Prayer has been called 'the heart of Christian spirituality'.[12] At the same time, it's probably the simplest aspect

---

[12] *Das Beten – Herzstück christlicher Spiritualität* (Prayer – The Heart of Christian Spirituality), United Evangelical Lutheran Church of Germany (VELKD), Hanover, 2005.

of spirituality. It doesn't require long-winded instruction: prayer happens, so to speak, of its own accord. Neither should we make it more complicated than it is.

Praying simply

In A *Simple Way to Pray*, [13] Martin Luther writes to his barber and good friend Peter Beskendorf, encouraging him simply to pray the Lord's Prayer. There's no need for elaborate prayers; the Lord's Prayer covers everything that needs to be said, so long as the heart is warm to it. Luther writes:

> Many times I have learned more from one prayer than I might have learned from much reading and speculation. It is of great importance that the heart be made ready and eager for prayer … What else is it but tempting God when your mouth babbles and the mind wanders to other thoughts?

And yes, prayer also demands concentration. It's good to find a special place or a particular time to set aside for prayer. In communal worship we pray together, but just as important is the personal prayer that happens in the course of our day. Prayer also requires us to learn a certain routine, which allows us to make talking with God a part of our everyday life. We open communications with God with a particular ritual, and then that conversation becomes a part of our lives, taken up at various other points in the day, or when we are at rest, or in situations of crisis or overwhelming joy.

Prayer needs a form of discipline, as well. If we only ever pray for particular things to happen, we're demoting God to the status of a slot machine, putting our little coins in and expecting answers to shoot out. Experience of prayer shows that the 'wish-fulfilment' issue is a problem that arises very early on. It tends to spring from a spontaneous impulse that arises in a particular situation of fear or hope. Prayer, though, is about persevering in conversation with God over the long term and thus becoming involved in a

---

[13] Martin Luther, *A Simple Way to Pray*, Westminster John Knox Press, Louisville, KY, 2000, pp. 30-1.

relationship with him – a relationship that will never leave us unchanged.

On the subject of prayer, the mystic Mechthild of Magdeburg wrote:

> That prayer has great power
> which a person makes with all his might.
> It makes a sour heart sweet,
> a sad heart merry,
> a poor heart rich,
> a foolish heart wise,
> a timid heart brave,
> a sick heart well,
> a blind heart full of sight,
> a cold heart ardent. [14]

According to Luther, the most important part of prayer is the 'Amen!' We must, he writes, say it with strength, to fight our doubts and hold fast to our faith. It means so much to me that Luther never swept doubt under the carpet. Nobody's faith is so sure that it never falters. Particularly when we suffer or see suffering, those pressing questions crowd in on us: is there a God? And if there is, how can he allow this? Why hasn't he heard my prayer?

What impresses me about the way our mothers and fathers in the faith experienced prayer is that, time and again, they brought their doubts into their prayers. There's a story of a group of pious Jews who, in discussing the merits and demerits of God, came to the conclusion that, given the state of the world with so much injustice and suffering, God could not possibly exist. Once they had come to this decision, the first thing any of them said was, 'Now let us go and pray to God.' It's stories like this that perhaps best describe the tension between faith and doubt. Of course we struggle. And time and again, we can feel that niggling itch that asks questions like: was this world really made by God? After all, everything can be explained differently! Yet these doubts

---

[14] In Jennifer Leigh Selig, *Thinking Outside the Church: 110 Ways to Connect with Your Spiritual Nature*, Andrews McMeel Publishing, Kansas City, 2004, p. 43.

– indeed, all questions – can be brought into our conversation with God. In the very act of praying, we are confirming our belief in God's existence.

Prayer spans the globe

I particularly like Luther's emphasis on the fact that we do not pray on our own: we are joined by all Christians everywhere. I find this thought that a prayer spans the world especially moving. We play our part in what you might call the orbit of conversation with God around the earth. This is another way in which God is present all over the world. The fact that we pray for each other all over the world places us into community with each other. Often, when disasters strike and we are moved to help, there is nothing direct that we can do, and yet we can pray for each other. As a bishop, I know that there are a number of parishes and monastic communities praying for me, and that often provides me with a great deal of encouragement. To tell somebody we are praying for them can provide comfort, help us share their burdens and encourage them through difficult times, because it lets them know that they have not been left alone.

In addition, there have been many times when people in other countries have told me how strengthened they feel through our prayer for them because of the knowledge that they are not forgotten, that someone cares about their suffering. We use the Ecumenical Prayer Cycle to pray for Christians in a different region of the world each week. [15] Prayer, then, is not just an element in my own relationship with God: it is part of our community. And if you ask whether prayer has any effect – it does, and it starts by helping us turn to God and to take responsibility for other people.

Fulbert Steffensky writes:

God is the first praying person: it is he who spoke the first word of longing. Who are we when we pray? What is prayer? To pray is to surrender oneself to the mystery of life. It is not a means to achieve an end: it is to surrender oneself to the mystery of life. It

---

[15] See Hugh McCullum and Terry MacArthur (eds), *In God's Hands: Common Prayer for the World*, WCC Publications, Geneva, 2006.

is when we pray that we are most the people we ought to be: not insisting on our own way but finding our expression in the one who is the foundation of the world ... We see our own beauty and worth in the eyes of God ... Prayer is the highest place of passivity, of the refusal to be our own lover or admirer. [16]

And that is the key experience of praying – letting go of ourselves. In praying, I am entrusting myself to Another. I am placing myself in conversation with God, who is so much more than here and now, who is wider and higher and deeper than I can imagine. And this surrender, this letting go, begins to characterize a whole attitude to life. In prayer, then, I experience freedom from all the pressure I am under. Many things lose their power to attack us when we express them to God. Prayer doesn't make problems disappear, but it can sometimes deflate them to their proper size. The burdens on our hearts and the fears that plague us don't vanish into the air, but prayer makes them manageable.

A Ugandan prayer
Keep us, Sovereign Lord,
From panic when crises and panics arise.
Help us to know that though you do
not always remove troubles from us
you always accompany us through them. [17]

Prayer changes things. The experience of Monday prayers at the Church of St Nicholas in Leipzig, Saxony, has always made a big impression on me. The meeting started as a small group in the days of East German communism, but it grew and grew and even outgrew the venue, for it provided a place where people could freely express their fears. It was the starting point for the 'Monday demonstrations' that helped topple the communist system. There is a novel

---

[16] Fulbert Steffensky, 'Die Schwachheit und die Kraft des Betens' (The Weakness and Strength of Prayer), in *Das Beten – Herzstück der Spiritualität*, Lutherisches Kirchenamt, Hannover, 2005, pp. 9ff., 12ff. (English translation prepared for this publication).

[17] 'A prayer from Uganda', in John Cardon (ed.), *With All God's People: The New Ecumenical Prayer Cycle. Orders of Service*, 2nd ed, WCC Publications, Geneva, p. 109.

by Erich Loest, *Nikolaikirche* (Church of St Nicholas), that provides a memorial to these prayers, which were initiated by Pastor Christian Führer. After East Germany's peaceful revolution and the end of the Berlin Wall, their moment of fame passed, but a small group continued to meet and pray every Monday. Then, once again, when the Gulf War began, thousands descended on the meetings in their desperation and fear. After that, the group returned to a smaller size but continued to pray. And when two men from Saxony were kidnapped in Iraq, people knew where they could go to express their care and concern. Once again, the Church of St Nicholas was a place of intercession.

When people are frightened or in danger and have no more answers, praying together offers security and community. One thinks, for instance, of prayers for peace, of the groups that met in silent prayer for the women who had been raped in Yugoslavia or of the events of 11 September 2001, when people poured into churches in their desperation and insecurity, lit candles and were thankful for the centuries-old tradition that gave them words to pray when they had no more words of their own.

Both personal prayer and corporate prayer, my prayer to God and my prayer for others, are thus fundamental pillars in Christian spirituality.

Suggestion

Find a rhythm for prayer that allows prayer and everyday life to complement each other instead of standing in opposition to one another – maybe by praying at the end of each day, placing the day and all that has worried or delighted you during it back into God's hands, or by saying a grace at mealtimes, thanking God for his gifts. Alternatively, simply take a specific moment each day or week to say the Lord's Prayer.

If you think you don't have time, or not enough, you may find these words of Teresa of Avila encouraging:

Prayer

Prayer can do anything.
   The moment you begin to pray, you feel your senses gather themselves like bees flying to the hive to make

honey. Do not believe that you would be more committed to prayer if you had much time. See your mistake: if you use your time well, prayer will not suffer. The most excellent kind of prayer and the kind that most pleases God is that which brings forth the best fruit – I mean, here, the kind of fruit that demonstrates itself by good works. [18]

The Tradition of Hymns and Song

If I were to give someone a sort of 'Christian survival kit' for their journey, the one item I would definitely include in it, alongside the Bible, would be a hymn book. Singing is truly central to Christian spirituality: in fact, music in general is one of the four supporting pillars of our faith.

It can do an enormous amount for us to have a song on our lips. Indeed, in the Psalms we are explicitly commanded to sing. Psalm 98:1 instructs us to 'Sing to the Lord a new song!' while Psalm 68:4 tells us, 'Sing to the Lord; sing praise to his name.' Lutheran churches have a rich tradition of expressing our faith in hymnody. Other churches, too, have a strong tradition of hymns and song. Methodists sometimes say their church was 'Born in Song', as one of its founders, Charles Wesley, wrote the words to more than 6,000 hymns, many of them still sung today.

Martin Luther himself was an amazingly creative hymn-writer. Another Lutheran, Paul Gerhardt, may well be the greatest hymn-writer ever. His hymns are among the most popular in the German Protestant hymn book, but they're also sung in Catholic churches and in other churches all over the world.

Gerhardt was born on 12 March 1607. Despite a hard life, he was able in his words to proclaim his confidence in his faith. His life was marked by many crises – he lost his job and outlived his children and his wife – and yet his lyrics hold suffering and the joy of faith side by side in such a convincing way that they still speak to us today. When we

---

[18] In Rosalies Taube (ed.), *Im Innern meiner Seele ist eine Kammer* (Deep Within My Soul There Lies A Room), Gütersloher Verlagshaus, Gütersloh, 2006, text for 14 October (English translation prepared for this publication).

get to know Paul Gerhardt's hymns we are reminded once again of the central role that has been played by song in the life of the Reformation churches.

Gerhardt's influence is vast, both on ordinary people amid often oppressive circumstances and on the 'greats' of German culture – Johann Sebastian Bach, Thomas Mann, Günther Grass, Gabriele Wohmann. His legacy is part and parcel not only of the story of our faith but also of our whole culture. And how are we passing this tradition on? Is there a song to be heard in our churches? A colleague told me that recently he's been simply playing CDs at funerals as nobody sings anymore.

It seems to me that we need to fight to save this tradition of Christian hymnody, which springs from the Reformation. It's sad to see how few people still know our hymns. The 2006 soccer World Cup may even have changed this situation slightly. Many people at least still know the words and tune of their national anthem – but then, that's a pretty essential requirement. Or we could point to political party conferences, where attempts to sing party anthems nowadays have to be propped up by a miners' male-voice choir. Or just think back to the last time you went to a wedding where the congregation wasn't used to singing. I well remember being scolded years ago by my youngest daughter, when she was twelve, at the dedication service at the start of the school year. 'Don't sing so *loud*', she hissed, 'it's *embarrassing*.' That was when I noticed that we were almost the only ones actually singing, apart from the pastor.

I want to encourage singing, and congregational singing in particular: song, too, lies at the very heart of spirituality.

Singing gives form, colour and words to our faith

Many of us know how it feels to have a heart overflowing with joy, or a heart that seems about to break with pain and worry. At these times, it is good to know a song. It helps to make space for feelings and questions of faith. I remember how my grandmother would always sing Gerhardt's hymn 'Commit thy way, confiding', even when she was in the kitchen making a stew. And I can remember one occasion when I was then able to sing through my tears, 'He points the clouds their courses / Him winds and waves obey / He will direct Thy footsteps / And find for Thee a way.' Yes: wise, old hymns can give shape, colour and words to our faith. However, new hymns can fill the same role. There is, for instance, a German soul artist called Xavier Naidoo, whose songs are not church songs, but whose lyrics often express deeply Christian beliefs. In a song called *Vielleicht* (Maybe), he sings, 'There is nothing more important than that connection to you / If I lost that connection it would be the end of me.' This is profound faith, given voice in new sounds and new words.

Singing is also one of the ways in which we – and especially our hearts – are built up. Johann Gottfried Seume, the German writer and poet, once wrote, 'Where there's song, there you may rest your head; / Where evil's done the voice of song is dead.' I'm not sure that that's always the case – one thinks of battle hymns and of anthems that pay homage to dictators. Let's not deceive ourselves: even music can be twisted, become exploited and allow that exploitation. But music also has that element of subversive freedom, for thoughts are free.

Singing helps us make the faith our own

Music also has that element of cultural edification. Mozart, Beethoven, Schumann – they are all names charged with meaning for anyone who plays an instrument or sings in a choir. The tradition lives on !

We need to learn anew that it takes more than intellectual thought to bring us to faith: we need to make it our own through all our senses. Church music is another form of religious education, and fundamental to it is singing. And since we believe that God rejoices when we sing, why not put new emphasis on our singing, in our nurseries and schools, our family services and confirmation classes, our worship and choirs ?

And I'm not only thinking of high culture. I don't believe that we in the church should simply throw out the serious music handed down to us. Yet sometimes, when I visit congregations at festival services, the church choir is joined by a gospel choir – and that's as it should be. It's another generation entering into faith in its own way. And of course, quality varies from place to place, and that's not something we should mock. Popular culture has its place in church. True, standards matter, but not every choir is going to sing to a professional level. The point is to experience the joy of singing and to give expression to our life and faith. Whatever their level, choirs sing to the praise of God and at the same time enrich and maintain the culture in our country. It's a community experience: 'Holy God, *we* praise your name.'

By contrast, when we turn our singing into too much of an expert educational activity, it can become exhausting. That is why I'm very happy to see that the desires of the people of our church have won out, and the latest Protestant hymn book in Germany includes such hymns as 'Silent Night', even if church musicians and even some pastors find them somewhat trite. We should not denigrate the hymns – nor any music – that have become dear to people's hearts: there needs to be space given to these feelings and emotions. Otherwise, we will be limiting ourselves to a restrictive and even elitist language of religious experience and inevitably curbing the joy of faith.

I recently read that the German neurologist and psychotherapist Eckhard Schiffer has demonstrated that, from earliest childhood, singing has a positive influence on health and learning ability. When we enjoy singing a song, our brains release an amount of 'happy hormones' equivalent to the amount released by seven miles of jogging.

Singing breaks down barriers

Singing also helps us learn about other cultures. The German Protestant hymn book now includes an Orthodox Kyrie and a setting of the Hallelujah from the Pacific, and we are so much the richer for that – even if these songs from the wider church sometimes sound very different when they are sung in our parishes from the way they sound in Russia, Africa or the Caribbean. Singing matters. As musicologist and singing teacher Karl Adamek puts it, when the act of singing is threatened, our 'souls are silenced'. People who sing are demonstrably healthier in mind and body.

Our Protestant hymn book in Germany contains more than just hymns: it includes the Confessions, Luther's Shorter Catechism and many different prayers. It's a compact compendium of the hymns and fundamental texts of Christianity. It's fascinating to read Luther's concise interpretation of the Ten Commandments and how, through the Commandments and the Confessions, he supplies us with the basic equipment for our Christian journey. When I am in a service that isn't catching my attention or where I'm finding myself becoming distracted, I sometimes flick through the hymn book to the index of authors' names at the back. And it amazes me that we still sing today hymns that people wrote over a thousand years ago, and use words first found by people to express their faith in the early 1600s.

Suggestion

Find a hymn book and flick through the index. Do you remember any of the hymns? Do any ring a bell – can you think of a time when you've sung them? I really want to encourage you to sing! If you think it's inappropriate or you feel embarrassed, go off into the woods. Hum; allow the sounds to start to form. Many of the hymns in the hymn book are available on CD – that can be a help in getting the hymns into one's head. Also: sing along in church; have the courage to take part. Powerful corporate singing can be a wonderful encouragement and create a sense of community.

Eight Arches of Tension

Anyone thinking about Christian spirituality needs first of all to abandon the notion that this is some kind of way of improving one's quality of life, something one can train for quickly or just 'buy in' when needed. These days there are a million and one spiritual 'wellness' products being hawked around on the market. Hotels offer special packages to relax your soul. Managers go on silence courses to help them face the stress of business. There are yoga courses for relaxation and tai-chi for inner balance. But, for me, the thing that sets Christian spirituality apart from this kind of 'wellness' spirituality is that it never loses sight of the 'world'.

Catholic theologian Johann Baptist Metz's assertion the Christian lifestyle is one of 'compassion' represents a vitally and fundamentally important point. Yes, the Christian lifestyle is partly about oneself, but most of all it is about one's 'elementary sensitivity to suffering'.[19] One look from Jesus enabled him to understand others' suffering. Our concept of 'sympathy' is not strong enough to express this. Metz writes:

> Compassion means perceiving and participating in another's suffering. It means actively considering the pain of the other person. Lastly, it means attempting to look at ourselves through another's eyes – even through the eyes of someone who has hitherto been an enemy – and holding that gaze for just an instant longer than our spontaneous reflexes of self-defence would like to allow. This mysticism, the mysticism of compassion, holds an incredible power of inspiration for our political life.[20]

To me, when we're thinking about spirituality, it's important to maintain the balance between love of God, love of self and love of neighbour. As I understand the Bible, Christianity never deals with any of these aspects by themselves

---

[19] See Johann Baptist Metz, 'Towards a Christianity of Political Compassion', in Robert Anthony Lassalle-Klein et al. (eds), *Love That Produces Hope: The Thought of Ignacio Ellacuría*, Liturgical Press, Collegeville, MN, 2006, p. 251.

[20] Johann Baptist Metz, 'Compassion', in *Was tust du, fragt der Engel: Mystik im Alltag* (What Are You Doing, Asked the Angel: Mysticism in Everyday Life), Bärbel Wartenberg-Potter, Herder, Freiburg, 2004, p. 39f. (English translation prepared for this publication).

but always with all three together. In our faith, we stand in a triangle of relationships between God, self and neighbour. This means that Christian spirituality is never withdrawn or individualistic; it is always rooted in the here and now.

In the Baltic Sea lies the island of Hiddensee. Over the front door of the manse on Hiddensee is an inscription that brilliantly expresses this tension between God's gift and our own responsibility: 'God is the wind and the waves. But the rudder and sails that bring you safe to harbour are your own.' Christian spirituality will motivate us and offer us opportunities. Indeed – to switch maritime metaphors – it anchors us and gives us stability. But it always points us back out into the world; it doesn't pull us away from the here and now, but rather opens up opportunities for life and action. This kind of spirituality strengthens our faith and gives balance to our life in order that we can speak up for truth and justice.

In many ways spirituality has become an ecumenical concept which points to the future, not least because spirituality helps us to stand in strength alongside our sisters and brothers all over the world. It makes the strong willing to stand up for the weak, and helps the weak know that they have not been left lost and alone, but that they are a part of the family of the children of God. This kind of spirituality gives people the power and the courage to confront injustice and violence instead of simply acquiescing to the status quo. It supplies the energy we need to break the cycle of self-centredness and to work at creating community. And that may be the biggest challenge that spirituality poses us in this age when every area of life is becoming commercialized. For me, it also represents that which fundamentally separates Christian spirituality from all these forms of 'me'-based spirituality.

The World Council of Churches assembly in Nairobi in 1975 spoke of a 'spirituality for combat'. Nowadays, we might find this concept a little harsh: spirituality and combat seem to us to be opposites. But if combat means gaining the strength to fight against destruction and violence, against the complete domination of the market, against alienation, then the idea does have meaning for today. We need a spirituality that enables us to resist evil. That's what will save our spirituality from becoming completely inward-looking. Christian spirituality is always interacting with reality – with everyday life and social challenges. It is a holiness inspired by God's Spirit, but aware of its responsibility to the world God has made.

There's an interesting illustration of this in the 2003 film *Luther*, mentioned earlier. In order to show the change that the Reformation brought, the film depicts a completely fictitious event. The young Luther buries a young man who had killed himself and performs the burial in the churchyard. Through this act, he demonstrates the unqualified, unconditional care and grace of God. In the film, Luther shows that even suicide is not beyond the reach of God's love. Instead of being buried outside the graveyard walls, as was the custom in those days, the young man remains part of the community of the children of God even in death. It provides a moving symbol of God's compassion for humanity, even in our deepest despair or most inescapable guilt. Luther's most fundamental insight about faith, that we receive grace freely from God, was the result of hours of Bible study, meditation and prayer – in other words, spirituality. But it showed itself in a life lived following Christ, which eventually brought Luther into conflict with both pope and emperor.

For me, the tension between spiritual and everyday life actually represents a very positive relationship in Christianity. I don't believe that true worship is to be found in total isolation from the world, nor do I think that the heart of Christian life is to be found in becoming completely wrapped up in this world. All Christians – indeed, every generation of Christians – need to find their own balance between the inner and outer life, between strengthening faith, and engagement with and responsibility for the world. In some cases, the pendulum will swing one way; in some it will swing the other. But no Christian can ever live completely isolated from the world, nor can they ever become totally enveloped by it. A spiritual experience of faith is not all about personal salvation, as so many sceptics would claim;

it is not about fleeing the world or retreating into the realms of the irrational. No, it means deepening one's experience of faith in a way that gives strength.

I'm going to explore and clarify this positive tension by using eight examples. Each begins with an imagined dialogue between me and different partners – four women and four men – all of whom have either made a significant contribution to spirituality in history or, in two cases, are fictitious characters who embody a way of living their faith that has proved its value in real life. My hope is that you will be able to recognize in these dialogues both the tension I have described and the relevance of spirituality for Christian life.

Prayer and Action:
A Conversation with Benedict of Nursia

Many see spirituality as a retreat from the world and think of believers as withdrawn from life, but I believe that faith unmistakably sends us back out into the world. In the account of Jesus' ascension, the angel sends the disciples, who are staring up at Jesus, back to Jerusalem. 'Why do you stand there looking into the sky?' he asks them (Acts 1:11): faith and action always belong together. Benedict of Nursia (c. 480–547) is widely seen as a pioneer of a form of monasticism that holds prayer and work in balance, providing an example for all Christians, in particular through his Rule, the Rule of St Benedict. [21]

You know, Benedict, that's quite a claim to fame – being the founder of Western monasticism! I mean yes, I understand when you say it wasn't quite like that, and how your thinking had been shaped by Augustine, Basil and all the Church Fathers, so it wasn't an entirely new invention. But all the same, it must have taken a unique talent to digest and condense all that you'd read and learned. Many people claim

---

[21] The *Rule of St Benedict* is still available. See, for instance, the English translation: Terrence G. Kardong OSB, *Benedict's Rule: A Translation and Commentary*, Liturgical Press, Collegeville, MN, 1996. There are also many commentaries, such as that of Anselm Grün, *Benedict of Nursia: His Message for Today*, Liturgical Press, Collegeville, MN, 2006.

your *Rule* wasn't really all that original. There are a lot of people who would say it only really reflects things that had long been recognized and lived as true. But you managed to take all these first creative steps and develop a 'hit' – a compendium, as it were. Even today, the *Rule* is still clear and persuasive; it has structure; it deals with the worshipping and the administrative life of the monastery; it encompasses everything from punishments to travel advice. That's still impressive today. Even twenty-first century business people find that interesting!

You tell me that in your day there was this desperate longing to be successful. I have to admit it reminds me a lot of my own time. You lived in a very uncertain time. The Roman Empire had fallen and something new, as yet unknown and unknowable, had yet to take its place. There were famines and epidemics and earthquakes.

You think you opted out of society? Tell that to the people who drop out today. You were clearly hurt by the collapse in morality. Today's drop-outs, on the other hand, are looking for freedom from the prevailing morality of our day. So anyway, you packed in your studies in Rome and withdrew to live in a cave. What must that have done to your parents? Such a gifted child, and suddenly he's living with these hermits, praying and meditating in cracks in rocks. Nowadays they'd have booked you in to see a therapist immediately. I mean, these were rich landowners, your parents. And then your twin sister followed suit – she's revered as a saint too now, by the way: St Scholastica. What was going on at home? Who was it who influenced you so? I would love to know.

But you can't have been all that isolated, really. They say shepherds and farmers used to come and see you. Maybe they were just curious; maybe they, too, were looking for what today we would call spirituality – spiritual nourishment. And then there were those monks who asked you to take on leadership of their little group.

'Huh', you retort. 'They just thought I was young and clueless. They weren't interested in maintaining monastic discipline – they were just a bunch of individualists. In the end they just wanted rid of me.'

What was it Jesus said to the disciples about shaking the dust off your feet and moving on? You certainly did that. Around 529 you and some like-minded men found the hill of Monte Cassino, between Naples and Rome. 'Yes', I hear you sigh. 'Finally we'd found somewhere we could live out in practice that balance of prayer and work.'

I think your principles of humility, obedience, poverty and constancy must have seemed just as daunting in your day as they do in mine. But even so, the lifestyle you created has clearly stayed compelling over the centuries – one might call it timeless. Nowadays we sum up your *Rule* with a phrase: *ora et labora* – pray and work. Now I know it wasn't you who wrote that – it was Benedictine brothers and sisters in the nineteenth century who coined the phrase as a sort of summary. To be honest, I like the longer version even better: *ora et labora et lege* – 'pray and work and read.' Amid all your different rules about prayer and how to run a monastery, how to live together, everyday practical provisions, dealing with infringements like lateness (!) and so on, I for one feel that Bible study gets rather a raw deal. Maybe I'm just thinking from too much of a Lutheran perspective. But, for all I value worship and work and even good order, the fact that Bible reading isn't mentioned until Rule 48 'On daily manual labour', which also deals with 'sacred reading', seems a little late on to me.

Yet your intentions ran much deeper than just maintaining order. On the one hand, you wanted us to hear God's voice, gaining focus through silence and through set times of prayer reconnecting ourselves to God throughout the day. I too believe these set rhythms are important – otherwise unimportant things inevitably crowd their way into the foreground. Although, oh my goodness: all those rules! How were members of your community ever supposed to express their individuality?

On the other hand, your monks were to work, so as not to lose their link to the world and to the earth itself. Now, this part really appeals to me: monastic life was not supposed to be divorced from reality. There were many who were astounded that you, a member of society's elite, would make physical labour such a foundation for life. But I'll let you explain.

'These days', you say, 'you'd probably call it living "holistically". I was concerned to give life some structure, some clarity and rhythm. Incidentally, I wasn't only thinking of monks. I often spoke about "the brothers" – these days I'd probably say "brothers and sisters". For my *Rule* could be a great help to the people living in "the world". They could often benefit from silence and prayer in order for their connection with their faith not to get lost amid the noise of everyday life.'

For many monks and nuns, your *Rule* is the most important book in their lives after the Bible. It's been published all over the world. And, even today, many people outside the monastic life find guidance in its pages. By the way, Benedict, many think of you as a peacemaker. The second motto of the Benedictine brothers and sisters today is *Pax* – 'peace'. I think that's because in your *Rule* you tried to regulate relationships between the generations and between the different positions of service from the abbot and prior right down to the porter. Sometimes rules can help to resolve disputes.

Yes, community was what mattered to you. You weren't interested in overwhelming people with high-sounding demands; you gave advice and suggested ways to resolve conflicts. You placed a lot of value on there being consultation within the convent, for instance. That doesn't sound like a withdrawn, solitary Christianity. For you, the monastic life, life in cloisters, was modelled on life in a family, with the abbot as father and all the monks as brothers. That's why your achievement was less to found a particular order and more to develop a conception of Christian life together with certain ground rules such as celibacy, eating simply and having set times for prayer, reading, work and sleep.

I think that balance between silence and community, between one's own prayer and connectedness to others is vitally important for Christian spirituality.

'Each person', you say, 'has to create a centre for their life by reckoning God to *be* that centre. That allows us to step out of the anxious prison of our own ego. After all, we are meant to be loving our neighbours, and only when we break free of our obsession with self can we be free to live for Christ and the community.'

Dear Benedict – when I think about what you say, it strikes me that it could be a helpful principle for today, too: to give our lives a centre that would make us free to be a strength for others.

Suggestion

Start the day with Luther's morning blessing:

I give thanks to you, my heavenly Father,
through Jesus Christ, your dear Son,
that you have protected me through the night from all harm
and danger,
and I ask
that you would also protect me today
from sin and every danger,
so that my life and actions may please you.
For into your hands
I commend my body, my soul and all that is mine.
Let your holy angel be with me,
and may the wicked foe have no power over me.

Love of Self and Love of Neighbour:
A Conversation with Elizabeth of Thuringia[22]

Love plays a central role in the Christian faith. The acceptance and experience of God's love are particularly vital in spirituality. But to talk of God's love for the world means refusing to accept injustice, war, hunger and poverty. This opposition to injustice is rooted in the Bible, as love for neighbour drives us to stand up for those who live on the margins. Elizabeth of Thuringia, also known as Elizabeth of Hungary (1207–31), is an excellent example of this for the way she devoted herself to

---

[22] This conversation is a slightly altered and abridged version of '… und die Hungrigen füllt er mit Gütern' (He has filled the hungry with good things) by Margot Kässmann, in Klaus Möllering (ed.), *Worauf ich hoffe* (Where My Hope Lies), Evangelische Verlagsanstalt, Leipzig, 2004, pp. 196ff.

*the poor. The daughter of King Andrew of Hungary, she was
betrothed to Ludwig IV of Thuringia when she was four, and
taken to Wartburg Castle in Germany (where three centuries
later Luther would translate the Bible into German). She married Ludwig in 1221 when she was 14 and the couple had three
children. Below Wartburg Castle, she built a hospital and visited the patients daily to attend to them. Elizabeth is perhaps
best known for the legend which says that while she was taking
bread to the poor in secret, her husband asked her what was in
the pouch; Elizabeth opened it and the bread turned into roses.
After Ludwig's death in 1227, Elizabeth joined a lay Franciscan group, but four years after her husband's death, she herself
died at the age of 24. Elizabeth gave of herself sacrificially to
help the starving and sick. At times, though, amid all her love
for her neighbours, she forgot to love herself. And yet we're supposed to hold the two together – indeed, Jesus saw the triangle of
love for God, neighbour and self as the greatest commandment.
Conversation with her is not going to avoid that topic, for in this
exchange also, the issue is once again finding the right balance.*

Dearest Elizabeth, I've wanted to talk to you for so long. I
attended St Elizabeth's School in Marburg, and I often used
to visit the wonderful Gothic church that bears your name.
It's Protestant now! After the Reformation, Count Philipp
of Hesse removed your bones and relics. It was time to end
the cult of the saints.

But we still heard the legends. For instance, the story of
the bread you were hiding that's supposed to have turned into
roses when your husband asked what it was – is that true?

You laugh?

You entered an arranged marriage at 14, and yet despite
that there seems to have been a happy rapport between you
and you husband. They say your husband was right behind
you, and even once said, 'Well, as long as she doesn't sell the
castle …' I like that; it makes me smile.

You know, on the one hand, I am hugely impressed by
your clear and undaunted passion to help the poor. Where
did you get it from? When you were taken to live in the
court of your future husband at the age of four, did you

already have that 'conviction'? Someone there must have helped you gain the confidence and faith needed. You did so much clear, tangible good for those living in poverty, and the cutting remarks you received from others simply didn't faze you. Christians are supposed to stand by the poor; in a sense, it's required of them; and you never wavered in putting this into practice. I can hear what you're saying – isn't that obvious to anyone who wants to follow Jesus? The thing is, though, you know well enough that it's not.

Your defence of the poor makes you a model for me. I often feel despair when I think of the thousands of people who are hungry, the many in places like Africa who are truly starving or living under the yoke of AIDS, while we here live in excess, although there is actually enough food for everyone. Sometimes I'll be standing in the shower and I'll think, what would a woman in Nigeria say to this kind of luxury? How am I supposed to tell a little girl in Ethiopia that there's enough food but the problem is how it is shared around? Why is it that in our wonderful, shiny, hi-tech, twenty-first century world, we can't manage to share out the food we have available? It has to be possible; it's fundamental to the future peace and justice of our world.

At this point, Elizabeth, I can hear you interrupting: 'Don't be so abstract! Instead, ask what you can do in practical terms.' And yes, you're probably right. But the world and its structures are complicated. That said, it was no different in your day. On the one side, there were the courtiers living in luxury in the castle while, on the other, people were living in misery in the streets. In the end there was nothing you could do about the structures, so you just eased the pain of some specific people. But even that's no small matter. Or maybe it's all about leading a consistent life, in whichever era we live.

A few years ago I attended the World Social Forum in Brazil. The forum was founded by a number of social movements as a counterpoint to the World Economic Forum in Davos. One might say that Porto Alegre is for the poor and Davos for the rich. People came from many different groups, including those without land, impoverished farmers, those living with AIDS and others. There was impassioned discussion of how justice might be achieved. They want to live side by side in solidarity. They don't have a single, comprehensive solution for the world's complex problems, but they refuse to give up the hope that another world is possible.

Was that your hope? Or was it more about you and your own faith? It annoys you, my saying that, doesn't it? And I can understand that it would. It's just that I always feel slightly uneasy when people think that they're going to do something good for the poor through charitable giving. It can so quickly become condescending and turn poor people into objects. For me, the best examples are the projects where homeless people sell magazines. Instead of sitting huddled on the ground asking for spare change, people are enabled to stand and meet me eye to eye as I buy a magazine from them.

Next you say, 'We have to please God with our lives.' Now this would be a great discussion to have, because that's a pre-Reformation position you're putting forward. It's exactly what Martin Luther was to rebel against 300 years later, when he said, 'No, God *already* loves us.' We don't need to try to earn our salvation through good works. It's not even possible. God gives our lives meaning and *as a result* we seek to live responsibly.

At the World Social Forum in Brazil, I felt something of the anger, the rage, that the poor feel towards the rich. And 'the rich' means us. One landless farmer asked me, 'How can you live like that, knowing that the same world order is killing other people?' If I explain that the system is so complex that direct help is all but impossible, you, of course, tell me that's just an excuse. In the winter of 1225–6, when a devastating famine whipped across the land, you, being a young countess, simply took money out of the state coffers to ease people's desperate plight. And (hats off to you!) you were only 18 years old! Now, it was love of the poor that made you do that, but wasn't it also hatred and contempt for those in power? For there was definitely also enmity and spite at court. Apparently, there were those who made you out to be wasteful. Did you have the inner strength to rise above all that, or did it hurt? 'I only cared to please my Saviour', you tell me. You say that now, but human beings need human relationships, too; we need to stand side by side in solidarity and work together if we want to change anything.

Dearest Elizabeth, you'll have noticed I said, '*On the one hand*, I'm hugely impressed.' Now I need to tell you my 'on the other'. What a high ideal you made of your own poverty! When you were 20, you wanted to sell all you owned and become poor yourself. I just wonder who that would ever have helped. Naturally, you reply: 'That was my own decision. It's not for you to judge. I wanted to be free of the burden of wealth.' And I do hear what you're saying. But is it not a slightly cynical attitude towards poor people? They'd love the security of knowing that they and their children would have a warm meal every day. 'All you think about is security!' you shout, and then quote the Bible: 'For what will it profit them if they gain the whole world but forfeit their life? Or what will they give in return for their life?' (Matthew 16:26). You're right, of course, but have you ever wondered what your actions mean for other people?

In the end, your confessor, the dreadfully strict Konrad von Marburg, prevented you from getting rid of all your belongings – though the pious old man probably had thoroughly worldly motives for that. 'That', you say, turning on me, 'is slander. You never knew him.' You're right. But from what I've read, I really don't like him. He was supposed to be your spiritual guide, but you let him humiliate you with penances and literal, bloody whippings. *I just don't get it*, Elizabeth. Did you *really* think that was what God wanted? What can God possibly gain from us destroying ourselves? It doesn't make any sense to me and I can't see anything spiritual in it.

Anyway, you invested your resources in founding a hospital at Marburg, caring for patients that no other hospital would take in. I think that's wonderful. The world is still full of that kind of need – and I don't need to go as far as Africa to find it: lonely old people whom no one ever visits; women ground into despair by caring for relatives. 'Then do something', you say, flatly. And that makes me admit: I could do more. And yes, once again, you're right to say I can't hide behind the excuse that there's nothing I can do to affect the complex, wider situation. It's true that we often allow ourselves to be put off by the fact that our opportunities for action are so limited, or even accept it, just too easily. So there you go: two-nil to you!

There's one thing that particularly concerns me, though. When you were 20, you entered a Franciscan order and gave your three children away. After the death of their father and being turned out of Wartburg Castle they must have been pretty thoroughly distraught already. Did you have to take your personal ideal of poverty so far that you would jeopardize your responsibilities to others? Because that's something I really don't understand. My care for my children always comes first – even before the church and my calling.

'I entrusted them to God', you insist. But do you really believe that your responsibilities towards your children are less important than your commitment to a good cause? Can we really refuse love and care to our nearest neighbour in order to do good to a more distant one? Now you tell me I have too romantic a concept of motherhood, it was different in those days – after all, you were sent out into the world when you were only four. But Elizabeth, every generation needs its strong characters! And they develop best when they can learn trust and love from their parents. I can see you think I don't have enough respect for the vows parents make at baptism. But those vows include the promise to bring our children up in the faith. That's not something we can delegate!

At last, on 17 November 1231, completely exhausted from your compassion and your sacrifice, you died. You were 24. That makes me so cross, because I don't see how it fits with Christian faith. 'Love your neighbour as yourself', said Jesus. That means I'm allowed to love myself! My body and my health are just as much a gift from God as anything else! How am I supposed to work for the poor if I've no more strength? Or maybe I'm just being too Protestant about it: by grace we have been saved, and not by works ...

Even so, Elizabeth, you're still a challenge. I often wish I could find a niche where I could make a clear, consistent, unmistakable difference for the poor. It seems too easy just to give money to an aid agency. It makes me lose heart to see this unjust world in which we live, where, to put it bluntly, half of us are too fat and the other half starve. And yet it's so hard to find solutions for the structures of world trade, power relationships, production issues, globalization …

Maybe the churches today really need to stress the fact that all people, wherever they live, are brothers and sisters, just as they were in Eisenach and Marburg. And maybe they need to hold you up as an example for your attitude towards wealth and towards holding onto personal privilege and possessions.

Yet I also see that God has set me in a particular place with my own responsibility. None of us can take all the sufferings of the world on our own shoulders. But Jesus' mission was to preach good news to the poor (Luke 4.18), and that he did in both word and deed. That's our job, too. If we as Christians want to be his followers, we must not let the issues of hunger and poverty drop off our agendas because we are too comfortable or the job is too hard. In that, Elizabeth, you're an example to me. 'I'm glad!' you say, and I'm happy that you're glad. I can well understand that you'd much prefer to be an example than a saint in a golden shrine. That wouldn't really fit with your life.

As concerns this self-destruction, though, I have the deepest sympathy for you and the purest rage for your counsellor. That's why I respect you as a mother in the faith, but I cannot honour you as a saint. The trust in God expressed by the Psalmist speaks more to me, when the Psalmist says, 'the hungry he fills with good things' (Psalm 107:9). I'm going to do all I can, in the knowledge of my own fallibility, to enable people to experience the words of that psalm coming true. For me, though, my capacity not to despair when I come to the end of what is possible or when I see my own failures has everything to do with my faith. I'm sure we'd agree on that, wouldn't we?

> *Suggestion*
>
> Love of neighbour is part of the Christian life. We're not all St Elizabeth; we can't all dedicate our whole lives to the poor. We need to take care of the responsibilities we have to our work and families. However, specifically supporting one project or becoming practically involved in one area is an important part of our lifestyle. It can mean supporting the magazine sold by the homeless people in our towns, making a weekly visit to an elderly neighbour who suffers with her health, becoming involved with helping children from the region around Chernobyl or helping with a local organization that provides free school meals for poor children. Look around and see what help is needed where you are or what initiatives already exist in fields where you can help. As the Taizé song says, *Ubi caritas et amor ibi deus est* – 'Where love and mercy are practised, God is.' Charitable actions, too, have their spiritual side.

The Cloister and the World:
A Conversation with Martin Luther

In the Middle Ages, those who entered the monastic life were thought of as being better people in God's eyes. They seemed to be living a life more pleasing to God, partly for having dedicated their whole lives to him, but also for denying themselves marriage. Ultimately, Martin Luther (1483–1546) rebelled against this, saying that nothing we can do or achieve can make our lives more worthy of God's recognition, but rather that we have value as human beings purely and simply because God first of all values us. Nevertheless, the monastic life still holds a special fascination and, even in the twenty-first century, looks like an opportunity to focus oneself fully on the most important questions in life, in contrast to a secular world in which so many people lose themselves. As a result, Martin Luther seems probably the best person to talk with about the tension between the cloister and the world.

Dear Martin, I wonder what you'd say if you knew that people are now seeking the monastic life once again? You were the one who quite deliberately kicked open the monastery doors and left.

'Now just hold on!' you shout. 'You people are misunderstanding me. What I always said was that we should reject the idea that the monastic life was an achievement, that it was a somehow "better" way of life. A lot of people were becoming monks or nuns out of fear, thinking that living in a monastery or convent was the only way they could be sure of God's grace. There's a legalism lying behind that kind of notion that I think is quite wrong. But to make that commitment in freedom, that's a completely different matter. I was already saying that around 1516, in my commentary on Romans – so really quite early on.'

True. And that's visible today when I read: 'Hence although all of these things are now matters of the greatest liberty, yet out of love for God each is permitted to bind himself by oath to this or that goal. But he is thereby no longer bound to these matters by the new law but by his own oath, which he has taken upon himself by reason of his love for God … But this must be done out of love and the faith that does not believe that he is doing these things as necessary for salvation but only of his own free will and out of a sense of freedom.' [23]

Could one say that your whole Reformation began from a question of spirituality? Ultimately, it was about repentance and for many people the experience of confession and forgiveness of sins is a profoundly spiritual one. To realize that my sin is forgiven can have an incredibly freeing effect. That's something I still experience.

'Oh, definitely', you say. 'It infuriated me the way the Church was quite literally selling the certainty of salvation. Out of sheer fear of punishment, people were letting Johann Tetzel, my first public adversary, and the other indulgence-peddlers steal the money from their pockets, on the grounds that they could even protect the dead from going to Hell. It was simply playing on the fears of anyone who wasn't celibate and didn't live in a cloister. That was what started it all, including my rebellion against the monastic life. God

---

[23] Martin Luther, *Luther's Works, Vol. 25: Lectures on Romans, Glosses and Scholia*, ed. Hilton C. Oswald, Concordia Publishing House, St Louis, MS, 1972, p. 489f.

forgives sins, not the Church, and he doesn't do it because somebody's bought an indulgence or has done this or done that, but simply because of grace! God says "yes" to us before we've done anything.

Yes, but you spent years in a monastery yourself. You'd promised God you'd become a monk if he'd save you from a storm. Why is it that you didn't find peace for your soul in that life?

You sigh. 'Peace for my soul? No chance. Not in that place. I couldn't sleep; I would turn all night, just thinking: there is no way I'm ever going to be able to live in such a way as to do all God demands of me. I'm not good enough; I'll never manage it all. And then it hit me, right there in the monastery: no one can! But God's not a tyrant – he loves me. Jesus Christ shows us that. Nothing that I do or achieve brings me closer to God. No, it's God who comes near to me, holds out his hand anew to me every day and forgives me. And that's the theology that later became known as justification by grace alone.'

Your spirituality's obviously also a critique of the way some people imagine they can approach God simply by much prayer, meditation or silence or, for that matter, by entering a monastery or convent, isn't it?

'In one sense, you're right', you reply, 'especially when people think they can achieve some kind of inner purity and make themselves sinless. I always remembered Christ and how it was the sinners he cared for. On the other hand, I always believed spirituality was important, just as long as it was centred on Christ: there's a kind of spirituality that I opposed all my life, which presents a kind of "natural" belief in God that tries to bypass God's revelation in Jesus. And I always said that God will always remain a God who is hidden, who can never quite be fathomed out. No meditation, no silence, will ever allow human beings to comprehend God completely.'

Did you know that someone has described you as the first 'Christmas Christian' of modern times?[24] Do you find that insulting?

---

[24] See Zimmerling, *Evangelische Spiritualität*, p. 54.

'No', you say, laughing. 'Because it's true, really: at the centre stands our loving God, who shows himself so remarkably in the story of Christmas. God came into the world for love. I once described God as a "burning oven of love". It's really not so much about teachings and doctrine: what matters is that God loves and wants us to love him. That's why spirituality's important for me: in faith I experience God. And in reality that's a process. It's not about *being* holy but *becoming* holy – and that requires practice, too.'

For me, though, there remains the question of whether this becoming holy, this focus on Jesus Christ maybe is better practised in the monastic life than in the outside world. I can see my question annoys you.

'It's a false conflict. I can miss God in the cloister or in the world. Or I can live, in the cloister and in the world, in a way that puts faith at the very centre of my life.' One might say that you democratized spirituality. When people know that they're loved by God, they will carry Jesus in their hearts, follow him and show mercy themselves. Those who entrust themselves to God are free to live and shoulder their responsibilities, either in the world or in the cloister. No longer is one more worthy than the other.

Dearest Martin, we need to discover this kind of freedom in our day, too. Many people feel trapped and sometimes want to escape; they feel under pressure or think their lives are meaningless. So many people long to feel this 'oven of love'. Yes, I think you can give us a lot of encouragement to put our trust in Jesus Christ himself and, through him, to find a way into life.

Suggestion

Create your own personal retreat space. You don't actually have to go to a monastery – although there are some wonderful monasteries that one can attend; it's just as good to create a space of this kind in your own home. It could be a stool for meditation, set in front of a cross, or an especially comfortable chair by the window – just somewhere that you can make time for your soul. It could even be a bench in the park. It just needs to be somewhere within easy reach, so that you can go there to find quiet for your conversations with God. Spending time with God strengthens our souls, gives us power and sets us free from the captivity in which we so often find ourselves trapped by the pressures of every-day life. It gives us the inner balance we need to see life in all its fullness.

Love and Pain: A Conversation with Mary

In Roman Catholic and Orthodox spirituality, Mary, the mother of Jesus, plays a special role. However, in recent years, she has also been rediscovered by Protestant churches. She represents that deep experience of love and pain that many people feel they share with her. While it is easy to see how love is part of life and part of faith, the dimension of suffering that also forms a part of that life and faith remains for many an experience that causes them to doubt and even, sometimes, to despair. Yet it is precisely in experiences of love and pain that many people feel nearest to God. The conversation with Mary that follows deals with this struggle to experience God.

I wonder whether you know, dearest Mary, how many people pray to you. I've always had a problem with that – I'm just too Lutheran. We prefer to pray directly to Jesus; Luther was quite specific about that. He believed there was no need to ask others – saints, priests or even you – to intercede for us, but that we could talk to God ourselves in prayer. I'm often struck by just how ubiquitous your image is, in all those different forms, all over the world. Along with pictures of the Crucified One, pictures of you with your son have been copied and copied down the centuries: you with the infant Christ, you beneath the cross and you as the mother with the body of her son in her arms. And people kiss your image and kneel before you and call out to you. There are even ten different days dedicated to you in the Church calendar!

You smile. 'Yes', you say, 'who'd have thought a simple girl from Israel could become so famous! Maybe the reason people invest so much in me is that they can understand my maternal feelings. Jesus often appears so self-assured. He sometimes gets presented as positively superhuman. To be honest, as his mother, I sometimes found that quite irritating – there's a few instances of that in the Bible. Maybe what really leads many people to feel a connection to me is the sheer spirituality of life itself. For instance, women who give birth to a child find it a spiritual experience, if they sense that this incredible process is a miracle from God. The resultant love for the child is a great mystery, and that's reflected in the many mother-and-child pictures. There's a real gentleness, even tenderness, to them. In situations of great joy you do feel God's presence; the divine comes very near. You can almost feel the Spirit that's moving.'

But you suffered so much as well. For me, it seems like the worst experience possible for a mother to see her own child die. 'Yes', you say, thoughtfully, 'but suffering's a part of life! And even in suffering you can experience God there, too. Because you think you can't go on and then you're given this ... this strength, and it enables you to grow beyond yourself. That was my experience and often I just had to stand amazed.'

That reminds me of something Dietrich Bonhoeffer once wrote – that God gives us the strength we need, not in advance, or we might become arrogant, but at the moment of need itself. 'That's just it', you say, 'and however much we may rebel against our pain, there's no such thing as a pain-free life. That said, though, I would still stress that God does not want us to suffer.'

Thank you, Mary. That means a lot to me. It horrifies me how people sometimes submit themselves to mortifications, humiliations, beatings and wounds because they think they're going to come closer to God through suffering. There have even been theological movements where people thought one ought to suffer as much as possible in order to become more like Christ. 'Now that I just can't understand', you say, firmly. 'Jesus brought light into the world so that people could have life in all its fullness. God wants life to be good!'

Yes, but Mary, there's still the horror of death. A lot of people today just shut their eyes to it, you know. They ignore their own mortality. My desire is always to integrate death into life, to see it as a kind of stage on the journey towards God rather than as the end point. What the death of your son has allowed me to understand is that his death, in particular, is not a full stop. The crux and the turning point of all Christian faith is resurrection and the defeat of death. That's why Easter morning begins with the cry, 'Christ is risen! He is risen indeed! Hallelujah!' The sad thing is that you don't always see much of this resurrection joy in the faces of Christians. Maybe there's a connection: death is so frightening precisely because our belief in the resurrection is so weak.

The medieval mystic Margaret Ebner once wrote:

> By God's goodness I was shown a sure way to everlasting life so that I could go to death as if to bed, without fright or fear, so great and strong was the divine trust I had in the mercy of God and so sweet my desire to enter into eternal joy. [25]

'Yes, but don't try and get there too fast', you warn. 'Death hurts. Your own death can be hard – leaving everyone behind. And it is often horribly painful to see the death of someone you love, or to be faced with sudden death. I do think one of the things that draw people to me is my tears of mourning for my son. They feel understood; they trust me, because I know from experience what suffering, grief, misfortune and despair really mean.'

You're also a symbol of compassion. It's in the way we see you bending over your son, both as a baby and as a corpse. 'The basis for it is always love', you stress. 'God can be experienced as love; God can be experienced through love. Time and again, God has been presented as this strict old man who makes a note every time we put a foot wrong and takes his revenge. That's a god to be scared of, a god to run away from. Experiencing God as love, as my capacity to love, on the other hand – that's not something we hear enough.'

---

[25] *Margaret Ebner: Major Works (Classics of Western Spirituality)*, ed. and trans. Leonard P. Hindsely, Paulist Press, Mahwah, NJ, 1993, p. 145.

You're right. Love, as a part of spirituality, is a whole topic by itself. There are many Christian texts in which love is depicted as an experience of God. For instance, Mechthild of Magdeburg, a member of a Beguine (a lay religious community) in the thirteenth century, accepted God's declarations of love and expressed them as follows:

> That I love you passionately comes from my nature, for I am love itself. That I love you often comes from my desire, for I desire to be loved passionately. That I love you comes from my being eternal, for I am without an end and without a beginning. [26]

This is a good, biblical realization. The First Epistle of John says, 'God is love. Whoever lives in love lives in God, and God in him' (1 John 4:16). Yet, just as with spirituality, we often see our experience of our relationships in terms of their usefulness to us: 'will they make *me* happy?' We lose sight of the fact that our relationships are also about other people – people who are different from us. The deepest expression of love is self-abandon, and that, Mary, is something people see in you.

'Possibly', you say. 'Relationship is always a process of give and take. But it is so hard to understand if it's not rooted in human experience. I can't understand what it means to say that "God holds me" if I've never been held by another human being. What's more, people still have a deep longing for relationship even if they've had no positive experiences of it. That's why it's so important for people to hear and experience the fact that *God loves them.*'

Mary, do you think you represent a special spiritual experience of women? I very often have the impression that women are more open to spirituality as something that is experienced. Men seem to need to hold more tightly onto what they know; the theology has to be 'correct'. I know that some men today *are* searching for something more, but, in many parts of the Church, if you talk about 'masculine spirituality', people just laugh. It's not taken seriously. And

[26] Mechthild of Magdeburg, *The Flowing Light of the Godhead*, trans. Frank Tobin, Paulist Press, Mahwah, NJ, 1997, p. 52.

if I give a blessing that includes women, they say that the idea of God as their Lord is missing. Perhaps you know this blessing:

> May the blessing of the God of Abraham and Sarah,
> the blessing of the Son born of Mary
> and the blessing of the Holy Spirit, who watches over us
> like a mother over her children,
> be with you all.

You like it, and that makes me happy. Often, I think the reason people are so scared of feminist theology is that it requires us to open ourselves up to new images and experiences. If God can be experienced as a *female* friend, as the eternal Mother, as a hen who gathers her brood under her wings (an image taken straight from the Bible – Matthew 23:37), that changes our understanding of God. Time and again, in reading old books, I've happened upon wonderful texts by women I simply never came across in my studies. Their experiences are so often swept under the carpet. That's how many women have rediscovered you, Mary, when they had previously seen you as a stranger because of all those pictures that make you look so far away.

You sigh. 'Yes, I'm pretty sure that has a lot to do with all that baggage about perpetual virginity – even though the Bible repeatedly mentions my other children. Another thing I don't understand is why so much has been added about me, right up to my being taken directly into heaven. Maybe you just need to relax a bit about all that. I think people just want to put me in this special box marked "inviolable, sacrosanct". That way they make me into this incredibly special person so they can offload all their love and their joy and particularly their pain and their grief onto me. But that's the miracle of the whole thing: I was only ever just a simple woman from Nazareth.'

And that, to me, is both comforting and encouraging: God is looking for totally normal people to show an imprint of the coming world in the middle of this one. God can be experienced right in the middle of life, of love, of loss. Spirituality truly is for every day!

Suggestion

Is there an image of Mary that made an especially strong impression on you? Try to find one. In churches, on altars, in secular art – images of Mary are everywhere, each one new and different from the last. What do people see in Mary? Is it the experience of love and pain, joy and sorrow? What experiences have you had in these areas? Do you feel love? Do you give love? Do you have worries? How do you deal with pain? Spending time in front of an image of Mary can provide a special place for tackling thoughts like these.

Images and Lives: A Conversation with Michelangelo

Images and colour play a major role in spirituality. Some pictures can transmit the truths of the faith in a lasting way. Immersing ourselves in a work of art or studying a picture intently can open up a new dimension in our understanding of God. For some people, meditating on a picture can give deeper meaning to their faith. Seeing the colours in a stained-glass window, for instance, can move our souls. For many people, the Sistine Chapel is just such a place – one that inspires wonder and an experience of faith. That's why Michelangelo, the artist responsible for its paintings, seems like the ideal person to discuss this topic with. He shows that images and colours of this kind are always being created and are in and of themselves an interpretation of the faith and a way of transmitting religious insight and experience. Thus, the image provides the meeting place for the spirituality of both artist and viewer.

What would you say, Michelangelo, if you could see the hoards of people who file through the Sistine chapel, staring at the ceiling, just to get a glimpse of what you created?

'I can hardly imagine it', you say. 'The process of decorating the chapel was dogged with bad luck from the start. Four members of our Swiss bodyguard were killed when an entrance arch fell in, two of my assistants died when some scaffolding collapsed, and then four passers-by died when some stones fell on them while we were walling up two windows. I was sure that the project had not been blessed by God.'

And yet it was! Even today, in the twenty-first century, those images and colours inspire people's faith. Don't you agree that colours and images, and art as a whole, are very often inspired by faith and in turn provide inspiration for faith?

'It makes me happy that my pictures are providing inspiration', you explain, 'but I was definitely not always all that certain in my faith. I often struggled with it. My mother died young, when I was only six, and I always missed her. When I moved to Rome in 1505, I was a restless man. The following year, the pope commissioned me to paint the chapel ceiling, but various things wore me down – the mould that grew over parts of my painting, irregular wage payments and a series of family problems. Then the pope went off on yet another crusade, which meant there was absolutely no money to be had anymore. By that point I was pretty disheartened about art and thoroughly angry at the Church.'

But I always thought your painting was an expression of your faith! You sigh. 'Well, the thing is, Pope Clement VII said he'd pardon my involvement as construction minister in the war against the Medici if I'd resume work on the Sistine chapel, and I thought, well, that's not a bad deal, is it? So it was more of a pragmatic decision, really. But then fate dealt me some nasty blows: my father died, as did a colleague with whom I'd been working for 30 years. That had an effect on me – it really left its mark. I painted right over some things and threw myself into finishing the chapel. The finished work definitely shows some of my inner struggle. Some people didn't like it, though, and soon after I died in 1564 they started painting cloths over some of the nudes. All I can say to that is, "No comment!"'

I can understand how that must be infuriating for an artist. I know how it makes me feel when people change what I've written. When I hear you talk like that, it makes me think what deep passions are brought out in people by guilt and forgiveness, pain and grief, and the question of good and evil. Our faith is constantly changing with our experience of life. Hugely significant situations like this cause some people to turn away from God entirely, for they feel abandoned, while for others it's precisely in these valleys that they experience God's presence and their faith grows deeper. So, Michelangelo, would you say these experiences strengthened your faith, and that this helped your pictures to communicate faith?

'Absolutely!' you say. 'My pictures told them the biblical story – just like altarpieces in churches. Now, when you tell a story, you're necessarily interpreting it – as a theologian you'll know that very well – and I tried to translate God's beauty, creativity and greatness into pictures. I wanted everyone who saw these pictures to be inspired in their faith and, through looking at them, to understand the wonder of God.'

Of all the images of yours that people admire in the Sistine chapel, it's the finger of God stretched out towards Adam that probably has the most profound effect on them. It's God coming towards a human being, God as a relational being, a God who wants to touch and to be touched. And thus man becomes the image of God. In that image, painting becomes theology and interprets the Bible.

I wonder what you'd think of today's art, Michelangelo. For many years, the art world has been in fierce rebellion against Church and faith, wanting to throw off its chains. And yet, even today, religious overtones and symbols are everywhere in art. Sometimes artists try to attract attention to themselves by producing religiously provocative work.

'Well', you say, 'art always deals with the fundamentals of existence. Art never exists in a vacuum; it always reflects the artist and the age they live in. Issues like birth and becoming, being and meaning, struggle and contemplation, death and resurrection are existential questions and they're therefore always what art's about. That's why artistic creations often have a religious dimension.'

I wonder where colours and images ought to belong in our spirituality. It says in the Bible that we should not make images of God, and yet art – including yours, Michelangelo – often depicts God.

'People need images', you explain, 'to fulfil their own power of imagination. God is more than any image can express; he can't be captured by a picture. But we have a need to illustrate him. Our image of God is often marked by our own life story. Whether it's the punishing father or the loving mother, we imagine God through images that relate to our own experience of life.'

But isn't that too narrow? Shouldn't we be defending God from being boxed into our little picture frames? One theologian has said, 'The prohibition on images exists to defend the vitality of life.'[27] 'Yes', you concede, 'we mustn't tie God down in pictures. But at the same time, people need images in order to grasp their own understanding of God and their deepening relationship with him. We mustn't allow God to remain an abstract concept. So, for example, God becomes tangible in the person of Jesus. And our experience of God can sometimes only be portrayed through images, or even simply through colours – warm, gentle yellow for the light that God brings into my life, or deep, dark red for the love that is God.'

Yes, I can understand that. There are painters whose works consist only of colours rather than actual figures, and they can create some quite remarkable, moving pictures. Even for those of us with less artistic education, colours like these enable us to express the things that move us. Indeed, today the trend is for abstract painting or even art that doesn't have anything to communicate at all, but which asks the people who look at them to come to their own understanding of what it means.

You sigh. 'I really find that hard to understand. But then I lived in a different time. My desire was always to convey something, to make things clearer, to reveal what was important and always to portray the greatness of God. Nothing was further from my mind than throwing up new questions.'

Can I ask you one last question? What do you think of meditating on images? It's become an especially important part of spirituality.

---

[27] Josuttis, *Heiligung des Lebens*, p. 62 (English translation prepared for this publication).

'Well', you say, 'it can be one way of approaching God, yes. I can imagine how meditating on an image can really help us to focus completely on God. But we do have to know what God we mean. What's the source of our image, what's our story? And that's what we find in the Bible. When you look at my pictures, you'll always be able to recognize the biblical allusions. But a painter's work will also necessarily reflect his own life story and that of the observer, and that allows us to draw spiritual inspiration from images when we can relate them to the biblical story, to the life of the painter or to our own life stories.

Suggestion

Take some time to visit an art gallery. Time and again in art, religion plays a role. Where can you recognize Christian motifs? Are they being employed in an unfamiliar way? Are they even being meant as a provocation? Where can you find depictions of biblical themes?

I always find it hard work to try to take in a whole gallery's-worth of art, but it can be exciting to look out for one biblical theme. For example, you could look into the question, 'Where does the cross appear in art?' Often, we can study a picture for ourselves and see how the artist has interpreted biblical themes, expressing their understanding and perception of them in colours and shapes. Some pictures move me deeply; some just irritate me. Time and again, colour and form can be a spiritual experience, which moves us, touches us, makes us think and rejoice.

The altarpieces in many churches provide a special way in. Today, there are also many of these to be seen in galleries. Artists have portrayed the biblical stories in so many different ways! Their work tells us so much of their understanding of the faith, and it can touch us so deeply and help us to think about our own understanding.

Personal Faith and Universal Responsibility: A Conversation with Elizabeth of Calenberg

We are always hearing calls for the Church to concentrate on 'the essentials' (by which people mean to stick to the faith) and to keep out of worldly, political questions. And yet believers live in the world; they cannot, nor should they, just opt out of it. Those who shoulder public responsibilities have just as much need to find orientation and guidance in faith as anyone else. Furthermore, those who have faith cannot remain untouched by the world: they will be committed both to passing on the faith and to the world itself. Faith does not absolve us from worldly responsibilities and spirituality is not a bolthole out of the world. Nearly 500 years ago, Elizabeth of Calenberg (1510–58) was one woman who tried to use her position of political responsibility to support the faith and, in particular, convents. She was married at 15 to Duke Erich I of Brunswick-Calenberg, who was loyal to the Emperor and the Roman Catholic Church. When he died in 1540, his and Elizabeth's son Erich II was not yet of age, and Elizabeth therefore became regent. Elizabeth's mother had been a follower of Martin Luther, and Elizabeth wasted no time in championing the Reformation. She maintained monasteries and convents, converting them into Protestant institutions, and established in Hanover an endowment fund that still today funds churches, social agencies and the sciences.

I've really wanted to talk to you, Elizabeth. You were such a strong, farsighted woman! I wouldn't have liked to be in your shoes, though – having to marry the 40-year-old Duke Erich I when you were only 15. Still, you were stubborn even then: you championed the Reformation in the Calenberg-Göttingen region.

'Oh goodness', you reply, 'Erich and I managed to come to our arrangements: he was always at Erichsburg Castle or at Calenberg Fortress; I spent most of my time in Münden. He had a mistress, though, and that made me furious. Anna Rumschottel, her name was. I once demanded he have her burned as a witch.'

Hmmm. Not very Christian really, that, was it? Still, I'm relieved you've proved me right. Erich did leave Anna, and the birth of your son must also have helped to bring some peace back to the marriage. But anyway, how did it come about that you converted to Protestantism?

'It all began with my mother', you tell me. 'She got to know Luther very early on – it was 1527 – even though my father did everything he could to stop her. I have to say the Reformation movement stirred something in me even then – it was blowing this whole new wind of freedom. In 1534 I went to visit my mother and met Martin Luther for myself. From then on we would write to each other. I would send him some cheese and wine and he once sent me back a translation of the Bible into German with a personal dedication! Luckily, Erich was very tolerant of all this, even though he remained a Catholic himself. After that, I summoned up all my courage and in 1538, for the first time, took the wine of Holy Communion, which in the Catholic Church only priests could drink.

That was more than just a religious affair, though – it was political, wasn't it? 'In my experience', you say, 'one can't always draw a nice clean line between faith and politics. After Erich's death, I really had to fight to gain guardianship of my son. In the years when I had political responsibilities, I used my power to support the Reformation. I brought in Anton Corvinus and a number of other men recommended to me by Luther. They were a great help.'

In Lower Saxony, where I come from, we hold you in high esteem – most especially, I think, because you saved the monastic communities in the middle of the Reformation. To this day, there are 15 orders and convents for women and three monasteries for men in my regional Lutheran church in Lower Saxony. Thanks to your wise foresight, the state authority for monasteries and convents responsible for running them still has enough money today to maintain these places of spiritual life. For it was you who, in 1542, decreed that all the church property that had been transferred to the landowners had to be managed separately and used exclusively for church, educational and charitable works. That has meant that, even now, it's possible to support spiritual life in some wonderful ways, including support for projects such as the youth church in Hanover or the Long Night of Open Churches, as well as in the monasteries and convents themselves. Many people get the opportunity to stay in them. There, they can learn anew how to be still and make spiritual discoveries; they join with others on their spiritual journey or learn anew how to be silent.

'You know, that gives me so much comfort', you smile. 'I felt quite embittered when I died: my son Erich had reverted to Catholicism and even had Corvinus arrested, and then my youngest daughter Katherine married the Catholic *Oberburggraf* Wilhelm of Rosenburg in my absence. But if these monastic communities remained, if women are still living in community with one another, if some of them are experiencing completely new spiritual growth – that, to me, is just the greatest joy. And so it's clear: political *nous* can indeed open up free space for spirituality. What's more, time and again, my faith gave me the strength to find my way in all the confusing paths of my time.'

You wrote some spiritual texts of your own, which was quite unusual for a woman in your day. 'Oh, nonsense!' you say, interrupting. 'It wasn't unusual at all. It's just that not much writing by women was kept. The powers that be didn't think it was relevant enough.'

No, you're right, much has been lost of what women of your day wrote. Nevertheless, your *Book of Consolation for Widows* is still well known and your advice to your daughter Anna Maria before her marriage to Duke Albrecht is still cherished as a marriage book to this day. You're also well known for your hymns. What's more, I think we'll rediscover more of your work in the next few years, when we commemorate the 450th anniversary of your death and then, two years later, celebrate the 500th anniversary of your birth. But it's the hymns that I find especially exciting.

'Oh yes, the hymns', you remember. 'That might have been the thing that most touched me about the Reformation – the way this singing imparted the Bible, the way the songs enabled us to express our new freedom, the way they gave us courage. I've heard that "A mighty fortress is our God" has fallen out of popularity these days, but for us it was a real battle hymn of the Reformation. You just can't improve on Luther's language in that hymn. Just the third verse alone used to give me the courage to face down every attack:

And though this world, with devils filled, should threaten to
undo us,
> We will not fear, for God hath willed his truth to triumph
> through us:
>> The Prince of Darkness grim, we tremble not for him;
>> His rage we can endure, for lo, his doom is sure,
>> One little word shall fell him.

(English translation by Frederick H. Hedge)

Tell me, though, Elizabeth, did you live to regret all your
involvement later, at the end of your life, when you were so
totally alone and abandoned, and when you saw your son
seemingly throw away everything you'd achieved?

'No', you reply. 'It was a hard thing to see, and I was
just incredibly sad for my children, but I'd learnt that God
would always stand by me, whatever happened. And even
if my whole life's work were to fall down before my eyes,
my life would still make sense. God puts each of us into a
particular place in history, and there we must freely shoulder our responsibilities. There's no shirking them. My duty
was to build the Reformation, while at the same time allowing space and opportunity for the monastic life. Well, I succeeded. And I'm thankful for that.'

So are we, dearest Elizabeth. We're thankful that we have
these wonderful monasteries and convents. It's not always
easy for them to find a form and place that's appropriate for
them in the twenty-first century, but interest in monastic
life is growing in completely new ways. Recent years have
seen a renewed growth of interest in living in a Protestant
monastic community, including among younger women,
and outsiders are welcoming the many opportunities the
communities offer to take time out. Thank you, Elizabeth,
for maintaining these communities. They represent a real
opportunity to develop and experience our spirituality in a
whole new way.

Suggestion

If you ever come to Germany, you will have a chance to get
to know the convents, monasteries and orders that Elizabeth saved. Today, they play host to many outstanding cul-

tural events. They share their great treasures through guided tours, concerts, readings, lectures and special exhibitions. For instance, there are the precious tapestries from the fourteenth and fifteenth centuries at the Kloster Wienhausen convent, or the copy of a thirteenth-century world map housed at Kloster Ebstorf. Kloster Marienwerder produces altar cloths. At Mariensee convent they teach traditional monastic embroidery techniques.

The primary concern of the communities of the convents and orders, however, is spirituality, and they offer a wide range of options in this area. They provide a space where those who are seeking can go to contemplate and be strengthened in their faith. The monastic communities of Wülfinghausen, Barsinghausen, Bursfelde, Mariensee, Marienwerder and Wennigsen offer diverse programmes, including opportunities to take part in monastic life as a short-term guest, 'oasis days' and days of contemplation and silence.

But you don't need to come to Germany to experience the spiritual resources offered by monasteries and convents. Maybe in the area where you live there are monastic communities, whether Roman Catholic, Anglican, Protestant or Orthodox that offer an opportunity to experience stillness and spiritual reflection.

Caring for Body and Soul:
A Conversation with Sister Susanne

I am certain that one aspect of spirituality is a 'spirituality of dying'. In her last book, German theologian Dorothee Sölle went so far as to speak of a 'mysticism of death'. Although she died before it could be completed, that text speaks of the concrete sensory experience of faith, of penetrating the most profound parts of religious experience through coming to terms with one's own mortality.

Every time I have visited or spent time with dying people it has been a deeply religious experience. All too often people deliberately avoid this experience, even though it will become a reality for all of us. And yet it is very common in a hospice to have deep experiences of faith in the midst of suffering. Experiences of this kind are also common among people working in hospice services. Sister Susanne is a fictitious character, but she represents a number of people with whom I've spoken about their experiences in hospice work.

I'm amazed that you cope with it – spending every day in the hospice with people who are dying, seeing death with your own eyes all the time. Does it not get a bit burdensome or depressing sometimes?

You smile. 'Well, people have different gifts. I've always been scared of talking to a big room full of people; I just can't do it. But holding someone's hand as they die, talking with them, moistening their lips, saying a prayer – that I can do. That's not a burden for me: it's just a wonderful calling. Here in the hospice, what we do is we help people make that final journey in dignity.'

But you only get the hopeless cases. Anyone in a hospice is close to death.

'Yes, but death *isn't* a hopeless case', you counter. 'Heinz Zahrnt said that, rather beautifully,[28] and here we see it proved all the time. There's so much life to be seen in death, if only we don't suppress death but consciously integrate it into life. We have this summer service, where patients' friends and relations come, and we sing together, and the sense of love and strength is so deep. Relatives of former patients who have died are present, as well as the people who work or volunteer here. It's not denial; it's a community of hope – hope that comes because we will not leave each other to go through death alone, and nor will we be left alone by God.'

Would you say that Dorothee Sölle was right to talk about a 'mysticism of death'? In the last few days of her life, she would argue with death directly, not knowing just how close it was to her. 'Dear Mr Death', she wrote, 'sometimes I suspect that love – in case we know what we mean when we utter this word – is the only thing you respect.'[29] Later on, she explained that God himself needed our comfort and our warmth and that we needed to be needed. She quoted Heinrich Böll, who'd once said that Good Friday was a day when we needed to comfort God. She continued:

---

[28] Heinz Zahrnt, *Glauben unter leerem Himmel* (Belief Under An Empty "Sky" – or "Heaven"?), Piper, Munich, 2000, p. 254.

[29] Dorothee Soelle, *The Mystery of Death*, trans. Barbara and Martin Rumscheidt, Fortress Press, Minneapolis, 2007, p. 2f.

Feminist theology proposes a new kind of thinking about God that necessarily leads toward a new kind of mysticism ... It says that God wants to be saved, that is, even a concept like that of salvation must be thought of in an ethical and theological context of reciprocity. [30]

So does a kind of spirituality of dying exist?

'Oh, I'm certain of it', you explain. 'People used to talk about an *ars moriendi* – an art of dying. I'm convinced that we need to relearn this *ars moriendi* if we're to be able to appreciate the *ars vivendi* – the art of living – in all its fullness. Being aware of one's own finiteness makes people more thoughtful and also, perhaps, more humble, and, at the same time, more joyful.'

A few years ago I watched the film *21 Grams* in the cinema. The film is about life and death, and its characters struggle with loss and guilt. The title comes from the claims of a researcher who said he'd discovered that people lose 21 grams in weight at the moment of death. He said that this was the soul. From your experience, Susanne, do you think there's such a thing as the soul? Because there are many people who wonder what's going to happen to them.

'My experience', you reply, 'is that we can perceive the soul. When a person dies, they don't go away straightaway. For a little while, something stays in the room. We always leave a candle burning in the corridor for as long as the body of the person who has died remains with us. To me, that's a beautiful little ritual. I would really like to encourage people to allow those close to them to die at home, and then not to shift them out of the house as soon as possible but to take that time to say goodbye – to take leave of their soul, we might say. From a purely legal point of view, we're allowed to keep those who've died with us for at least 36 hours before the undertaker comes. (Incidentally, there are also hospice services who visit people at home.) And there's a beautiful liturgy of farewell before a body is put in the coffin. There's a pastoral value in being aware of what we are doing when

---

we do this: it does the living good to say farewell in an intentional way.'

For me, the soul is that which makes each person different, that which makes them who they are. The prophet Isaiah said, 'I have called you by name, you are mine' (Isaiah 43:1). That's quoted at every baptism service, and it also means that God knows every person by his or her name. We never lose this unique identity, even after death. This belief is what makes Christianity distinct from other religions, where the aim is to lose oneself in the great whole like a drop of water in the ocean.

'Yes', you say, 'I agree with you. My experience has been that people each have their own individual way of dying. Some people suffer horribly – less with the pain, since nowadays we can reduce pain to a minimum with palliative medicine, and more because they can't let go. The thought agonizes them in the truest sense of the word. Some people relive the hardest times of their lives – war memories and so forth. Others just slip gently out of this world and into God's future in their sleep. And there are others who seem to make this quite definite, conscious decision that it's now time. I knew one old lady who arranged everything, sorted out her will and her funeral, and wanted to see her daughter one last time, and then just as her daughter had left, said, "Right, that's that, then", closed her eyes, and died.'

I'm reminded of the words of the Apostle Paul, that none of us lives to himself or dies to himself. 'If we live, we live to the Lord, and if we die, we die to the Lord; so then, whether we live or whether we die, we are the Lord's' (Romans 14:8). What that means is that in both life and death we are held by God: we remain in God's blessing even through death.

'That's how I see it, too', you affirm. 'That's why being with a dying person is a thoroughly spiritual experience. Because when you're sitting there, holding someone's hand, you have the space and the depth to think about life and death yourself. You search for prayers you can say or songs you can sing. And many a time I've seen a person who's capable of hardly any movement at all any more start to move her lips to join me in reciting the 23rd Psalm or the Lord's Prayer, for instance. Those are words that have burned their way deep into the person's soul, so deep that they're even present in death. It often also helps those who are close to the patient to go through that with them: they're often terribly frightened of death because they've never seen a dying person before.'

So accompanying someone in death is also good for the spiritual well-bring of the people close to them?

You explain: 'Of course, sometimes it's frightening and oppressive first of all. That's why we're always available for relatives to talk to. That includes explicit spiritual care. It also includes crying, tears and grief – because death does hurt, especially when we love. It's probably always easier to say goodbye to an old person, because we can say, with Psalm 90, "The days of our life are seventy years, or perhaps eighty, if we are strong" (Psalm 90:10), but when a young person dies, there's always anger, and rage, and the big question, *Why?* And then we all suffer together; it's impossibly painful – so much life unlived. When someone dies young, it's always especially painful for those who loved them: then they really need spiritual care.'

But, of course, we don't have an answer for the *Why?* My thought is that God doesn't work us like puppets – indeed, we all want to be free ourselves. But, for that reason, we can't hold God responsible when we're hit by illness or accidents.

You sigh, Susanne. 'Well that's all very well in theory', you explain, 'but in practice people get angry at God, and I think that's perfectly normal. What's more, God allows it – just look at the Book of Job in the Bible. In fact, I think it's *right*: in the middle of our grief and our rage, we have to stay in contact with God. Indeed, maybe our link to God is never stronger than at times when we face up to dying and death. It's such an essential experience because it brings us especially near to God and gives particular meaning to our hope of resurrection. And for this reason, it's not an experience we should avoid. Dying takes time; grief takes time, a time of caring for body and soul.'

Thank you, Susanne. Talking with you has shown me once again that there is a very deep spiritual experience – an experience of God – to be found even in death and in spending time with the dying. And thank you for the peace and the time that you give to the dying and those close to them. The service you give, you give in the name of all of us. You and the many others who work or volunteer in hospice care, telephone counselling and other areas – you're not just helping those directly affected; I believe you're also making a contribution for all of us together, for all of us as a community. Caring for those whose souls have been hurt helps to keep the fabric of our community together.

Suggestion

Spend some quiet time in a graveyard. Graveyards can often be places of rest in every sense of the word. There are echoes of human lives to be sensed in the dates or inscriptions on the headstones of strangers, and when graves belong to people we've known it can awaken our memories. A cemetery is a good place to reflect on life and death, to sit on a bench and even gain a glimpse of our own death. Do we suppress our thoughts about dying, or do we dare to give them space? Are you ready? Have you arranged what needs arranging and said what needs saying, just in case your death is sudden? And in case your death is slow, have you made a will, or a 'living will', for instance? Do you know a place where you would like to die? Have we made someone our executor? It's important – and, for those we leave behind, massively helpful – to have taken the time to consider these things, which we all too frequently ignore or avoid amid the pressures of everyday life. Coming to terms with our own mortality can bring new depth to our life in the here and now.

But it's not just practical questions that matter. The most important questions are the spiritual ones. Can I trust God, even in death? Do I see that my soul is held in God's hands? Can I let myself go in the love of God, or are my feelings ones of deep fear? We need to take time to come to terms with these feelings. I am certain that there is such a thing as a spirituality of dying, and that the mysticism of death is very real.

The Hope and the Struggle:
A Conversation with Pastor Enrico

I'm often struck by the extent to which spirituality has been individualized in Germany. Indeed, we can sometimes use spirituality as nothing more than a way to shut ourselves off from the problems of the world. And yet, in the 19 years that I was a member of the Central Committee of the World Council of Churches, I had many opportunities to visit churches overseas, and I was struck time and again by how an unqualified commitment to justice was seen in those churches as part and parcel of the life of faith. Spirituality is not an add-on extra: it is something lived out in the real world and inextricably linked to the fight against poverty, hunger and oppression. Pastor Enrico is a fictitious personality, but he represents the many Christians I've had the chance to talk with in Africa, Asia and Latin America.

You know, it's been really good to visit these projects with you. But I wonder: how do you cope seeing all this injustice before your eyes every day? I mean, here are the landless, there the big landowners; here are the expensive villas, there the poor favelas. And the work you do with people who've lost their land, for instance – there's no end to it! When I saw the pitiful figures on this scrap of occupied land, the faces of the children stamped unmistakably with hunger and hopelessness, I just thought, where does one even start?

'Yes', you say. 'There's a lot of injustice. In my years living in Germany I almost forgot that. It often makes me so angry, I want to kick doors down and scream. And sometimes it makes me feel just completely helpless, because I can see that everything I do is no more than a drop in the ocean. But, at the same time, I've learnt to be patient and take things step by step. Being there for people with love and giving them back a sense of their own value – these are what's most important. And beyond that – well, it's just important to fight injustice. Injustice must be called by name, on that we will not compromise.'

Does that get you in trouble? 'It depends with whom you mean', you say. 'Of course, even here, there are a lot of Christians who think that our commitment to the poor shouldn't really extend beyond charity. The Church, they say, should keep its nose out of political issues. But I just *know*, when I read the Old Testament prophets and hear their thunderous rage against injustice, and when I see the biblical visions of justice and peace kissing each other, that justice is more than merely a pretty word – it's our mission.'

Indeed, Jesus said that when we visit those in prison, feed the hungry or invite the homeless into our houses, we're doing it to him.

'Quite', you reply, 'and that tallies with my own experience. When you commit yourself to the poor, you experience God for yourself. Not because you're being this amazingly generous person by sharing your food – that'd just be putting yourself on a pedestal – but because, suddenly, you feel love, you receive it, and you're enabled to give it. And it's an overwhelming experience: suddenly, it's not about giving and receiving anymore; it's about truly becoming the *familia dei* – the family of God.'

The World Council of Churches assembly in Nairobi in 1975 spoke about a 'spirituality for combat'. Do you think that's a good way of thinking about it? Many people in the West felt quite the opposite: spirituality, they felt, had more to do with spiritual matters and couldn't be related to ideas of fighting.

'That's something that worries me about Europe and other rich countries', you interject. 'Christian belief in your part of the world is fast becoming a private matter – just something for Sundays and special festivals – and your spirituality becomes nothing more than some nice icing on top of the cake. For us, faith is about life and death: it's about children living on the streets, those living with AIDS who can't get medication, little girls whose bodies are just rented out to tourists. In our world, saying that everybody's equal, everybody's made in God's image, everybody has a right to food, shelter and education – that's a declaration of war. I think our faith gives us the strength to carry out that fight.'

In the 1970s, liberation theologian Ernesto Cardenal used to hold discussions about the Bible with farmers on Nicaragua's Solentiname Islands. I found them quite fascinating. I was enthralled to read how these people, who couldn't read or write, were interpreting the biblical stories and bringing out of them deep truths that I'd never seen before.

'It still is fascinating!' you exclaim. 'And why? Because those are exactly the sort of people that Jesus spent his time with. Fishermen and tax collectors and whores. And he said to those people: God loves *you*. These were people who'd grasped the freedom of the children of God. And that very quickly became a threat to the political and religious status quo.'

But hang on, though, are you not becoming a bit nostalgic now? The greatest days of liberation theology seem to be behind us. The kind of churches that are really on the rise here in Latin America are the Charismatic movements, the Pentecostal churches, small, individual congregations and cults based on African or indigenous ethnic traditions.

'That is true', you say, thoughtfully. 'But I'm convinced that this individualism, where it's all about *me* and *my* salvation, will not last long term in our context. For one thing, a lot of it's managed through fear: if you don't do this or that, you're in danger of facing the wrath of God. That's almost the same as the clash that came in Luther's day. Moreover, Pentecostal churches are also beginning to understand that practical action and love of neighbour are part and parcel of Christianity. And anyone who loves his neighbour cannot ignore injustice. Pentecostal congregations have been setting up social projects for a long time now – Rio de Janeiro's *Fábrica de Esperança* (Hope Factory) is just one example. So, for me, liberation theology is not just a thing of the past. It remains a challenge for the present, and we have to take it forward into the future. You can't do theology in an ivory tower! When I read articles or books on theology from the West, I often get the impression that that's just what you're trying to do – to pretend you live in an ivory tower far from war and hunger and injustice. But faith has everything to do with real life!'

What would you like to see Europe doing?

'You need to get away from your self-centredness. It really looks to me as though you still think of yourselves as the centre of the theological world, but there's far more exciting theology to be found in the world today: the reflections of Dalits in India on the meaning of the Christian message within the caste system, for instance, or the way Christians in the Pacific are thinking about the theology of creation. What's more, the way you do church in Europe has long since ceased to be an example for us. You have to become more alive and get closer to life. If you're having spiritual experiences in meditation and stillness that's great, but something has to come out of it. You can't just say, 'Well, I've found my relationship to God; the rest of the world can worry about itself.' Faith is always about giving us the strength to face the world head on. If you really see us as your brothers and sisters, you can't hide yourselves away in your own context and your own little world. If there's going to be globalization, then let's have a globalization of justice!'

Thank you, Enrico. You're right: the Church continually needs to broaden its horizons to see the whole world.

Suggestion

Many churches or church districts are twinned with parishes abroad. This allows a direct contact that enables the building of relationships that go beyond charity and make learning together a real possibility. It's also possible to support specific projects through church development agencies. Spirituality is never an end in itself; rather, it's something that we live and experience in a real world of real challenges. Talking with Christians from Africa, Asia and Latin America can broaden the horizons of our faith and overcome our provincial mindset, and we can discover new dimensions in our spirituality. These relationships formed across the world are fundamentally enriching for the ecumenical existence of churches.

Sixteen Ways to Start:
Basic Tools for Spirituality

So how can I test spirituality out in practice? How does one begin? What's the best entry point for me?

I think if you're interested the best way to start is quite simply and practically to have a go at one or another of the ways to practise spirituality that are on offer. This part of the book introduces 16 such ideas. It doesn't claim to be the final word, although it does deal with some very varied aspects of spirituality, from extremely broad aspects of experience such as light down to very practical ones such as making a pilgrimage. In order to avoid making any value judgements, I've arranged the various options in alphabetical order. There is, however, a great deal of overlap among many of these opportunities and ideas. Light or a picture can form part of a meditation. One might have a mystical experience while spending time with creation. A fast might take the form of silence. That's why this book can only offer suggestions – a brief outline to show the sheer diversity of spiritual options.

Nobody is going to be able to fully comprehend and put into practice every single one of these ideas. Each of us has different sensibilities and ways of perceiving things physically and of thinking about our faith. You need to work out for yourself what forms, places and starting points work best for you and what will make up your own spiritual journey. All I can do here is to briefly outline some ideas and give some practical advice to help you get started. I've also sought out an inspiring text for each section, for poetry is probably the most beautiful language of spirituality. Some of the texts will bring a smile to your face, and that in itself is good for the soul. If it hadn't been the poems, it would have been images or sounds or a soft rustling in the air. Sadly, such things are rather hard to convey in a book like this, but they can be found everywhere in life. Furthermore, there is a wealth of opportunities for discovering the route for one's own spiritual journey in many congregations, monastic communities, retreat centres and other church foundations.

Commit yourself to searching for your own way to experiencing God. I don't believe there's any 'wrong' way to do that, as long as the four foundational pillars are solidly in place. When Jesus Christ is the centre of our faith – where, to speak metaphorically, the cross stands firm – there is also room for creativity and diversity. Another reason that many are sceptical of spirituality is that it represents a risk: it requires us to give ourselves up to our faith. We can no longer maintain that distance that even a church service allows us to keep. Sometimes it takes courage to commit oneself to a journey of this kind – but it is a courage that pays off, for a lived, experienced faith brings a depth to our lives that simply cannot be bought.

It's a depth that has to do with security and guidance in this life, yes, but also so much more. To find time for this in our life, to create space for it, is a rewarding business. In this way, we are able to learn to see life in all its God-given fullness. We experience the reality that Christian faith is not just a matter for the intellect to be comprehended in our heads, but something that can be perceived by all the senses. And so the biblical record becomes a personal experience of God; and so we can experience Jesus Christ with hearts, and hands, and voices.

Angels

Many people believe they have encountered an angel at some point in their lives. It may be a guardian angel, protecting them in times of severe danger. People can become angels for others: the nurse who cares for us, the friend who holds our hand, the neighbour who brings cakes, the brother who listens. And angels can bring God's good news, such as the angel who announced to Zechariah the birth of his son (Luke 1), or the angels in the field who told the shepherds what had happened in Bethlehem (Luke 2).

It took me a long time to appreciate angels. But I do have a few figures of angels in my office. They've now been with me for quite a while. Symbols like that can stimulate a conversation. Sometimes I'll say to one of them, 'What are you thinking now, then?' And suddenly that creates an interruption in my daily routine, a moment of deeper reflection. I've also experienced angels in my life: people who were there for me when I needed love or care, or who simply listened when I needed an attentive ear. I can think of one angel who once brought me a wonderful bouquet of roses at a time when I was feeling quite disheartened. He did me a power of good, although he had no idea of it himself.

My favourite reference to angels in the Bible is Psalm 91:11: 'For he will command his angels concerning you to guard you in all your ways.' Those were the words sung by the Hanover Bach Choir, to the setting by Mendelssohn, on that day in 1999 when I walked up to the pulpit at my installation as a bishop to give my first sermon in my new ministry. At the time, I thought, 'What can possibly go wrong now, if his angels are protecting you?' Of course, even angels are no substitute for good preparation! But they do stand at our side, representing God. They offer us the gift of an experience of the presence of God. Whenever we feel God beside us, or the gospel suddenly becomes clear to us anew, that's an angelic experience. Angels enable us to discern God's existence – indeed, they simply remind us that *God is there*. They are also a spiritual phenomenon.

There are some wonderful stories on this subject and some wonderful books on angels, some that take us through the year [31] and some that make us smile. There is one book in which several people tell of the security they received in their lives from a bronze figure of an angel. [32] It's good to start by looking at the biblical accounts of people's encounters with angels, such as that between Mary and Gabriel in the first chapter of Luke (starting at Luke 1:26). You might want to find a figure of an angel that resonates with you. There are some wonderful pictures of angels, as well as figures made from wood, clay and all kinds of other materials. Of course, they're only symbols, but sometimes, when an angel figure of that type catches my eye, it leads me into talking to God. 'Let your holy angel be with me, that the evil foe may have no power over me', said Luther in his morning

---

[31] For instance, Anselm Grün, *Angels of Grace*, New York, Crossroad Publishing, 1998.

[32] *Ich geb dir einen Engel mit – Erfahrungen mit einem Symbol* (I'm Giving You An Angel: Experiences With a Symbol), Andere Zeiten, Hamburg, 2004.

and evening prayers. An angel figure can remind us of the God in whom we can trust day and night. It speaks to us that God is there. And through that, it might open our ears, our eyes or our heart to become sensitive to the fact that there's more in the world than we often see.

> *The Angel in You*
> The angel in you
> rejoices over your
> light
> weeps over your darkness
> From his wings rush
> words of love
> Poems' caresses
> He guards
> your path
> Turn your feet
> angelward
> *Rose Ausländer* [33]

Blessing

'I will bless you ... so that you will be a blessing' (Genesis 12:2), said God to Abraham, as he sent him on his journey, showing the double direction of blessing: as we ask for God's blessing, we also bless others and become a blessing to them. Blessing is a turning to God and a pronouncing of his presence, experienced by us and passed on to others.

There are many formulas for pronouncing a blessing. The most familiar is that known as the Blessing of Aaron, so called for Aaron and his sons, whom Moses instructed in the way they were to bless the people of Israel:

> The Lord bless you and keep you;
> the Lord make his face to shine upon you, and be gracious to you;
> the Lord lift up his countenance upon you, and give you peace. *(Numbers 6:24–27)*

---

[33] Rose Ausländer, 'Der Engel in dir' (The Angel in You), in *Ich höre das Herz des Oleanders. Gedichte 1977-1979* (I Hear the Heart of the Oleanders: Poems 1977-1979), S. Fischer, Frankfurt am Main, 1984 (English translation prepared for this publication).

This is the blessing usually given in German Protestant churches to the whole congregation at the end of a service. It promises the people that God will be with them and strengthen them when they return to their everyday lives at the end of the service. Many people also feel themselves protected and cared for through blessing. Since becoming a bishop, I've done more blessing of others than I have received blessings, but I notice how good I feel when someone offers me a blessing.

In worship, we give a blessing to the whole congregation, but there are many occasions in our journey through life when we receive blessings as individuals. We receive a blessing at baptism, at communion or confirmation, at our wedding or when, after we have died, our body leaves our home for the last time. In addition, there are services of blessing where people can go forwards by themselves and have hands laid on them in blessing. Sometimes I'm asked to perform that kind of individual blessing myself after a service: some people might ask for a personal blessing before a journey or a stay in hospital.

But the act of blessing is not something that's restricted to church services. We can all pronounce a blessing over someone as they leave on a journey. For instance, I've been in airport chapels when one member of a family has been going on a long journey to somewhere far away, and the whole family has prayed a blessing over the person who is leaving. I was in a hospice once and saw the sense of freedom with which a woman was enabled to die after I had pronounced God's blessing on her. And we can send one another verses of blessing: many of these are currently highly popular, especially those from the Irish tradition.

Blessing is a spiritual experience in that it enables us to feel our lives being held by God and the love of other people. The promise that we will remain in God's circle of blessing gives us strength in hard times. It can be a healing experience to allow the awareness of this blessing to penetrate down to our very hearts. Blessing is about having 'life in all its fullness in every part of human existence'.[34]

---

[34] *Evangelischer Erwachsenenkatechismus*, p. 603 (English translation prepared for this publication).

Have a think: who would you like to bless? Who may badly need to have a blessing spoken over them? A blessing can be especially beneficial for the sick, the lonely and the dying. Or you could take on the blessing that comes in the service in a conscious way. If you're facing a particular situation in your own life, think who might be able to bless you. You can ask a pastor to bless you – though all Christians can pronounce the blessing of God.

An African Blessing

May the Lord bless you.
May he make your feet dance
and your arms strong.
May he fill your ears with music
and your nose with sweet smells.
May he put a song in your mouth
and joy in your heart.
May he bestow on you ever anew
the blessings of the wilderness:
stillness, fresh water and new hope.
May he give us all ever anew the strength
to give hope a face.
May the Lord bless you.

Creation

The Bible is full of descriptions of nature rejoicing. The mountains burst into song, the streams bubble up with praise to God. This is something that can be hard for us twenty-first century city dwellers to grasp, strangers that we have become to nature. And yet nature isn't far from us. We don't need to travel far and wide to find it. Every one of us can reach the edge of some woods easily. And it can be an uplifting experience to go there, breathe deep, hear the rustling leaves and see how the dance of growth and decay carries on without our help.

What's important is to feel wonder, to pause and take it all in consciously. Even in our hi-tech world we still know how it feels to be overwhelmed by a sunset, struck by the sight of a rainbow, overcome by the sheer power of a storm. These kinds of experiences of nature have led many people to think of God, feel his presence, and offer a prayer.

Jesus often used nature to draw out analogies. Probably the most famous is this one:

> Consider the lilies of the field, how they grow; they neither toil nor spin, yet I tell you, even Solomon in all his glory was not clothed like one of these. (Matthew 6:28–29)

Rushing waters, mighty fires, storms over the sea – the Bible repeatedly uses elements of nature as images of encountering God. Today, as well, nature can be the place where we find God. Now, of course, I certainly don't think that nature can be an alternative to church. We mustn't say, 'I prefer to seek God alone in the forest than in a church building'. For church is a public place of community, and our worship together is one of the fundamental pillars of our faith. And yet, nevertheless, we can experience God in and through nature, just as Paul Gerhardt wrote:

> Go forth my heart and seek delight
> In all the gifts of God's great might,
> These pleasant summer hours:
> Look how the plains for thee and me
> Have deck'd themselves most fair to see,
> All bright and sweet with flowers.

Praise of creation turns to praise of its Creator. Francis of Assisi expressed this process in a way that has made a great impression on many, many people in his 'Song of Brother Sun':

> May you be praised, my Lord, with all your creatures,
> especially brother sun,
> through whom you lighten the day for us.
> He is beautiful and radiant with great splendour;
> he signifies you, O Most High.

To Francis of Assisi, the sun is an allegory of its Creator and he uses it to praise him. For this thirteenth-century monk, the same was true of 'brother wind' and 'sister water'. His prayer is infused with the recognition of how an appreciation of creation can bring us to an awareness of God. And out of this awareness there flows, as a result, an awareness of how we treat this creation.

Let me encourage you to open your eyes to nature. Far too often we simply don't notice the changing colours of the leaves, the infinite beauty of a seashell, the way the ocean calls to our heart, the wonderful rustling of branches in the wind. Far too often, in our day, the sounds of nature are simply drowned out.

> Should our soul catch sight of something beautiful and sweet,
> it thinks, how beautiful and agreeable and good
> is the one
> who has made it,
> And so it is drawn straightway to the One who created
> all things.
> Should it hear a sweet melody or some other sound
> to which it thrills, it thinks:
> Oh, how wonderful is the voice,
> that calls you,
> from which all gracefulness and all melodiousness
> proceeds.
> And so the soul will seek the One in all things
> until it gently feels something of the sweetness of God.
> And whatever creature our soul may choose for its amusements;
> it always keeps in mind God's delight,
> creating us for this beauty, joy and entrancement
> so as to release and move all
> to the knowledge and love of his goodness.
> Mechthild of Hackeborn [35]

Dance

Once, at a Protestant church convention, I was invited to speak in a meeting on the subject of spirituality. The meeting ended up being an event in which I and 7,000 others were expected to perform liturgical dance. Now, of all the gifts God has given me for my journey through life, I really wouldn't say dancing was the greatest. Yet that was a moving afternoon – in the truest sense of the word. I'm terribly aware of how critically some view this approach to spirituality, seeing it as being all about women with pretty ribbons. But that's

---

[35] In Rosalies Taube (ed.), *Im Innern meiner Seele ist eine Kammer*, text for 5 February (English translation prepared for this publication).

a view born of fear and short-sightedness. The body is a gift from God, and it can be a wonderful and godly experience to enjoy that body, to put it in motion, to express our pain or our joy with movement. Far from being ridiculous, it's spirituality – it's lived, experienced faith.

I would love for us to rediscover movement and the joy of movement. It's very much like sport, which also fails to receive the emphasis it deserves in the Church. When we dance, our body is filled with the potential to express our love, our sorrow, or our love for God. Physical gestures are very expressive signs. Communications experts discovered a long time ago that, for instance, the German Chancellor should not be irritated if the French President kisses her hand, but should make sure she signals their equality by gently placing her left hand on his right upper arm. Just think of someone taking the time to work that one out! And I'm not saying that to be ironic – it just goes to underline the significance of physical movements and gestures.

I also want to encourage you to see that physicality and sport are not un-Christian. We shouldn't be worshipping our bodies, but, through sport, we do learn to become more consciously aware of our body as a gift from God. Sometimes when I'm running, for example, I can feel the rhythm of my breath following the rhythm of my feet, helping me to let go, empty my mind and become available for new thoughts and experiences.

Dance can help in the same way. I find it very moving to see children in a nursery giving expression to God's love through the movements and gestures that accompany a song. They're so unselfconscious and enthusiastic. Adults often look at this kind of thing rather critically, but it's a wonderful thing to know how to use physical movements to express ourselves – both for our joys and our pains! Eastern cultures have gestures of this type that seem to be significantly more universally understood, culturally rooted and practised, such as pounding the chest with the hand to signify grief, for instance, or stretching one's arms to the heavens.

Christianity and dance, liturgy and the body – these are not mutually exclusive. Our religion and our worship are far too often top-heavy and brain-focused. Pastors preach about sorrow as though they are reading the notices, or a text that puts joy into words is read in a voice that conveys indifference. Introducing physical movement at a time like that can bring the text's meaning to life. Let's not be scared! Jesus Christ did so much through physical gestures: for instance, when he drew the children to himself and showing them as an example to follow, he must have gone down onto his knees.

So, can you find your own dance?[36] There are services you can attend that will help you. However, it can also be good to practise it by yourself. How can you express the joy of the Lord? Which gestures of prayer do you find helpful? And what do you do with your body in times of grief and pain?

The Lord of the Dance

I danced in the morning when the world was begun,
I danced in the moon and the stars and the sun,
I came down from heaven and I danced on the earth
At Bethlehem I had my birth.

'Dance then, wherever you may be
I am the Lord of the dance', said he,
'and I'll lead you all, wherever you may be
and I'll lead you all in the dance', said he!

I danced for the scribe and the pharisee,
but they would not dance and they wouldn't follow me.
I danced for the fishermen, for James and John
they came with me and the dance went on:

'Dance then, wherever you may be
I am the Lord of the dance', said he,
'and I'll lead you all, wherever you may be
and I'll lead you all in the dance', said he!

---

[36] See, for example, Manfred Büsing and Holder Kiesé, *Tanz Gebärden Haltungen: Schritte zu einem bewegenden Gottesdienst* (Dance, Gesture, Attitudes: Steps Towards Worship That Moves), Lutherisches Verlagshaus, Hanover, 2000; Bodo Leinberger (ed.), *Getanztes Leben: Heilende Liturgie* (A Dancing Life: A Healing Liturgy), Wort im Bild, Hammersbach, 1993.

I danced on the Sabbath and I cured the lame;
the holy people said it was a shame.
They whipped and they stripped and they hung me on high,
and they left me there on a cross to die.

'Dance then, wherever you may be
I am the Lord of the dance', said he,
'and I'll lead you all, wherever you may be
and I'll lead you all in the dance', said he!

I danced on a Friday when the sky turned black
it's hard to dance with the devil on your back.
They buried my body and they thought I'd gone
but I am the dance and I still go on!

'Dance then, wherever you may be
I am the Lord of the dance', said he,
'and I'll lead you all, wherever you may be
and I'll lead you all in the dance', said he!

They cut me down and I leapt up high;
I am the Life that'll never, never die;
'I'll live in you if you'll live in me; –
I am the Lord of the dance', said he.

'Dance then, wherever you may be
I am the Lord of the dance', said he,
'and I'll lead you all, wherever you may be
and I'll lead you all in the dance', said he![37]

Fasting

Fasting is enjoying a renaissance, not only in the area of spirituality but also in the form of fasting for health. Christian fasting, however, is never an end in itself, but rather provides a time of preparation. The best-known period for fasting in the Christian tradition is Lent, but people used to fast during Advent, for instance, to prepare themselves to celebrate Christmas. Friday is a day of fasting; people go without meat in memory of Good Friday. Fasting, then, has a role to play in maintaining the rhythm of the Church

---

[37] Sydney Carter, 'The Lord of the Dance', in *Rejoice and Sing* (full music edition), Oxford University Press, Oxford, 1991, pp. 292-3.

year. In spiritual terms, fasting is understood as a time of self-denial. In physical terms, it can make us aware of how narrow our habits are, how something like a glass of wine can taste very special when we've been without it for a while, or how totally used we have become to the television without noticing the extent to which it determines how we arrange our day.

One way we practise fasting in Germany is the 7 Wochen ohne initiative of the Protestant Church.[38] The initiative, whose title means 'Seven weeks without', was the brain-child of a group of journalists and theologians who, in 1983, decided one night – following a pub crawl – to fast from Ash Wednesday until Easter. Today, more than two million people take part every year. The aim is to become aware of what we are doing when we observe Lent. *7 Wochen ohne* invites people:

- to reconsider their ingrained daily habits;

- to deny themselves certain 'sins' that they enjoy, such as alcohol, nicotine or sweets;

- to become aware of what really makes up the quality of life;

- to make space for change;

- to develop new outlooks;

- to show solidarity with disadvantaged people through refusing to be a consumer.

It's exciting to see the experiences people are having for the first time thanks to this tradition, and I can only encourage you to try fasting in this way: not as an obligation but as a way of experiencing new horizons, as a journey of discovery. The *7 Wochen ohne* initiative also sends out Lent letters throughout the seven weeks to those fasting. This means that they're not fasting alone. They're part of a community of people sharing their experiences. That alone is valuable.

---

[38] www.gep.de/7-wochen-ohne.php (available only in German).

The *Fastenbegleiter* or 'Lent book' is a wonderful book where people are able to write their own experiences of that fasting period. In it, author and church musician Siegfried Macht tells this story:

> Mr P. was once asked by his neighbour why he fasted. He answered, 'An old work colleague of mine once had to move out of his large apartment and into a small one. He threw a lot of stuff away that he couldn't take with him, and kept only what was most beautiful and most useful. It wasn't long before he was able to move again, but never have I seen a more tastefully furnished and decorated flat in all my days. Since then, I've tried to move house more often.'

That story helps us to understand what fasting is about. When I fast, I'm sorting out what's important in life and what isn't.

What I don't like about fasting is how quickly a new legalism can emerge: I can't do this; I mustn't do that. I love taking part in *7 Wochen ohne*, but it's important for it not to become too moralistic. Fasting should be an experience of freedom, not constriction. I always find it a relief to read how monks used to allow themselves exceptions throughout the fast – on Sundays, on journeys and so on. But it remains true that fasting is about taking stock of myself: am I free from dependence on certain foods or habits; can I break out and change things, change myself? It can be a really liberating experience to realize that maybe I don't need certain things so badly after all. And that freedom gives me the space to open myself up to new experiences of myself and faith.

Many people's experience is that fasting lends a whole new meaning to the Lent period. It's a special time in the year, and when we fast we really become aware again of what it means. This is especially true in Holy Week, from Palm Sunday, through Maundy Thursday and Good Friday, up to the celebration of Easter itself. When we fast, we take time to take on board these accounts from the Bible, which are so central to the Christian faith. We are stepping into great traditions, entering into profound experiences. That's the way to find our roots.

Letting Go
Now there are many people,
Who give up things out of love,
even holding in high regard
the things they have given up.
But the person, who truly recognizes,
That it counts for nothing if they give up
themselves and all things -
yes, the person who so loves,
truly possesses all things.
All of the disorder
within and without
is rearranged in the detachment,
In which one gives oneself up,
And gives oneself to God.
Meister Eckhart

Icons

In Orthodox churches, icons play a major role in spirituality. I was once visiting an Orthodox convent, and I asked the abbess how she helped all the young women who'd grown up without Christian instruction to grow in understanding of their faith. I was expecting she'd talk about Bible study or introductory courses to Christianity. No, no, she said, they didn't have any of that, but every girl was given an icon for her room. She explained, 'You don't need to read the Bible; you just need to look into the eyes of your icon, and there you find the whole of faith and the whole of the gospel.'

For a Lutheran Christian, that's difficult to accept. We strongly believe that faith comes from the Word of God, and from hearing and reading that Word. And yet icons and images can also be a way to sense God and deepen our experience of him. Now, according to my way of thinking, that can only happen alongside the Bible. But I accept that it's different for other people, and that there's definitely something we can learn from the love of icons. There were apparently massive disputes within the churches of the East in the eighth century regarding the biblical ban on images, but the argument that God had put on flesh himself in Jesus Christ carried the day, and the portrayal of Jesus – and therefore God – in images was permitted.

Protestant and Catholic Christians are no strangers to images such as those that tell the stories of the gospels. Many a church altar does this – and does it strikingly. The meaning of icons, though, is somewhat different. They're seen as 'images that give an authentic representation of Christ, Christ's completed work of salvation, the saints and their lives and – in later times – dogmatic "truths".[39] I had to begin by understanding this. Icons aren't about transmitting or teaching doctrine, so to speak, nor are they about telling or illustrating stories or giving counsel – although that's how I usually see images used in Christianity, such as those created by Michelangelo. Rather, they really are literal representation. For Orthodox believers, icons represent the presence of God, which is why they kiss them and venerate them.

In my office hangs a copy of the famous Icon of the Trinity by the Russian painter Andrei Rublev, which shows the visitation of Abraham by three angels on the plains of Mamre (Genesis 18). The Bible passage in question has traditionally been interpreted as referring to the Trinity. This icon, for me, is an extremely moving symbol of the Trinity. The three angels – or the Father, the Son and the Holy Spirit – are in conversation together, in relationship with each other. God is no solitary, isolated being; even within himself he is already a set of relationships, a community. Yes, it's only a picture, but it's also a spiritual encouragement – to meditation, to reflection, to the strengthening of our faith.

Rowan Williams, the current Archbishop of Canterbury, has written a wonderful and highly accessible little book that provides an introduction to icons.[40] I found it a help in approaching icons. In a very careful and easily understood way, he opens a path into experiencing them for Western Christians.

---

[39] Karl Christian Felmy, 'Ikone/Ikonenmalerei' (Icons and icon painting), in *Religion in Geschichte und Gegenwart (RGG)* (English translation prepared for this publication).

[40] Rowan Williams, *The Dwelling of the Light: Praying with Icons of Christ*, Norwich, Canterbury Press, 2003.

If you'd like to enter into the process of creating icons in a highly personal way, there are courses and introductory books teaching how to paint icons yourself. You can also buy them. They can be found on posters or bought over the Internet, or you could even have an icon painted for you individually, although the waiting lists for those stand at two to three years. These are the kind of icons painted by Sister Eva-Maria in St Hildegard's Abbey in Rüdesheim, south-western Germany, who says that, for her, painting icons is 'a symbol of one's own life: you choose a way of life, but that life changes as it grows. So for me it was a very natural journey, and every time I make an icon I feel – and I've felt this so many times now – that something is happening both within me and through me, like the process is a gift.'

Gazing on an icon is a first step. It can help us go deeper into the texts of the Bible; it can move us to meditation; it can remind us to place our days into God's hands.

John of Damascus, the Church Father, wrote:

Of old, God the incorporeal and uncircumscribed was never depicted. Now, however, when God is seen clothed in flesh, and conversing with men (Bar. 3.38), I make an image of the God whom I see. I do not worship matter, I worship the God of matter, who became matter for my sake … I will not cease from honouring that matter which works my salvation.

Keeping Silence

Many people have found silence a difficult practice to master. We use words all the time as we talk about everything and more – including much that doesn't need to be said. Silence is hard to learn. Then there are those to whom silence is too familiar, because they're lonely, because nobody speaks to them. Silence of that kind is hardly a spiritual experience. Rather, what is spiritual is a conscious decision to forego speech for a certain amount of time – by spending just one day alone in silence, for example. Making a decision of this kind often leads on to deeper self-reflection. We cease constantly expressing everything in words; we are alone with ourselves.

The thirteenth-century Abbot Bernard of Clairvaux once wrote a letter to his contemporary, Pope Eugene III, himself a former monk, counselling him not to devote his energies entirely to other people. In it, he wrote:

> How can you ever fully and truly be human if you have lost yourself? You are human too. If you are to complete and perfect your humanity, you must have a considerate heart, not just for all others but for yourself, too. For what will it profit you if – as the Lord said (Matthew 16:26) – you gain everybody else only to lose yourself? Give yourself a break. I don't say, 'all the time'; I don't say, 'often'; but I do say you should give yourself a break, just once in a while. Be there for yourself, as you're there for others, or, at the very least, *after* you've been there for others.

In my experience, silence is also helpful in finding oneself in this way. Silence removes me from the expectations of other people that I must respond to them, find words for what's in my head, have something to say, take action. I may take an hour of silence. I can snatch a short period of quiet by, for example, finding a church and going in to pray. We can build silence into travelling; it can be part of meditation or reflection on a Bible verse; it can be a healing interruption in our daily routine or a conscious ritual in its own right.

Silent retreats in monastic communities are becoming more and more common. While many people come out of such experiences remarking how hard they found it to learn silence anew, they always report that it did them good. Those who spend time in silence become more aware of what they say. You only have to watch some of the chat shows on television, where guests simply prattle away without any deliberate choice in the words they use, to see how devoid of content so much talking is. Silence makes our speech more deliberate.

Whether just for a moment, for an hour, for a day or for longer, being silent is always a breaking away from a daily life marked by talking. It can bring us closer to God, teach us to hear his Spirit, and simply allow us the space for a spiritual experience.

Being silent suited me so well
that, when I did not speak,
it lent me a special peace,
and I was able to overcome all adversity with grace.
I also enjoy being alone,
and it vexes me to have to hear any external noise at all.
Margaret Ebner

Light

Light has a special role to play in the Christian faith. Jesus Christ said, 'I am the Light of the world' (John 8:12). John's Gospel repeatedly uses this contrast of light and darkness as a symbol for the reality of God. In the Old Testament, too, light is used as a symbol for God's existence and creativity: 'Then God said, "Let there be light"; and there was light' (Genesis 1:3).

Perhaps the most beautiful way of symbolizing this light and making it visible and tangible is to light a candle. We light candles on the altar when we worship together. Each week in Advent, we light another candle as we journey towards Christmas, until Christmas Eve, when the tree represents the arrival of the Christ Child. Many churches have an area for intercession, where we light candles as we pray for other people. When we remember those who have died, we light candles for them as we keep their names alive by speaking them out.

I remember light being used in a very special way at a children's event that I once led in Hofgeismar in central Germany. On Easter Saturday we lit a pre-Easter bonfire, as is the German custom. At the end of the evening, we took a light from the bonfire and carried it into the little chapel in the academy cellar. The children watched over the fire through the night in shifts, until, at five in the morning, a little procession of them made its way from the chapel into the church. One after the other, the children each lit a candle, and light diffused throughout the church, until eventually, as day dawned outside, the silence of the night was broken and the place resounded with the celebration of Easter.

In this way, candles can deepen what our faith means when it says that Jesus Christ is the light of the world: he's the light of hope in the darkness, amid our worries, questions and pain. Lighting a candle invites us to reflect, to pray, to meditate. Find a place – in a church or a chapel or at home – where you can experience for yourself, in your own way, the warm light of that flame.

Other forms of light, however, also help us to trace the significance of Christ. 'The light shines in the darkness', says the first chapter of John's Gospel, 'and the darkness did not overcome it.' God himself comes to the world. Every morning we're reminded of that with the sunrise. As it did on the first day of creation, the light displays anew God's presence and his desire to participate in the world. And deliberately watching the day begin can lead us to an experience of that presence and desire. As the hymn says, 'Morning has broken'.

Once, when I was on holiday with my youngest daughter in a tiny village, she turned to me and said, 'It's never this dark at home in Hanover!' And she was right. In our cities and towns we simply don't know what deep darkness looks like any more. The blackness of night simply doesn't penetrate our brightly lit houses. Maybe that's why we don't notice the light enough.

Take some time to watch a sunrise. It's a way of helping ourselves understand anew what Jesus Christ as the Light means for us, our lives and the world. That light is the light of the Creator, who promised that day and night would not pass away as long as the earth remained. It's the light of Easter morning and of the Resurrection that brings light to our world, for, as the Book of Revelation says, pain and fear and death will be no more.

Who are you, Light, who fills me up
And brightens all the darkness of my heart?
You lead me like a mother's gentle hand
And, if you let me go,
I'd know not how to take another step.
You, nearer me than I am to myself
And inward more than my most inward parts.

And yet ungraspable, unholdable,
Evading every name:
Holy Ghost – Eternal Love.
Edith Stein

Meditation

My first encounter with meditation happened a number
of years ago. I had intended to pop into a service of Lenten
devotions. The children were waiting for me at home, so
I was somewhat pressed for time, and I had thought it
couldn't go on longer than 15 minutes. How wrong I was!
The pastor asked us to kneel on meditation stools, placed a
picture of Christ in the middle of us, and read a short biblical text. Then she asked us to take 25 minutes to meditate
on the text while looking at the picture. I quietly fidgeted
and fumed my way through the first 10 minutes. Thoughts
hit me from every side: 'I wonder if I could just leave? The
kids will be wondering where I've gone! I don't know why
I even came here in the first place ...' But after a while I
noticed I was able to leave that all behind. It was as though
I became empty, and I was enabled to focus my thoughts on
that picture of Christ in a whole new way.

We can meditate alone or with others. It can be a profound experience of togetherness to sit in a small circle, read
a text from the Bible and reflect on it together. On the other
hand, I find that a meditation stool in front of a cross or a
picture in one's own home also works very well; we can
then absorb a picture or a word from the Bible and meditate
on it. Experience shows that it's helpful to have set times for
meditating. It doesn't need to be long, and it doesn't need
to be every day, but it is important to keep a specific period
of time free.

You can't just step out of your everyday routine, have
a quick meditate and then be on your way. It takes time
and rhythm to find that quietness. It scares me sometimes
just how hard I find it to let go, to put everything spinning
around in my brain onto one side. I can only manage it if I
truly make time for it. Personally, I prefer to meditate on a
text from the Bible. A good method for me is to read a psalm

or the daily reading and then to spend 25 minutes kneeling before a cross using a meditation stool.

There is another, beautiful meditation idea called the Pearls of Life.[41] Originating in Sweden, the Pearls of Life consist of a small bracelet with 18 pearls strung on it. Each pearl has a meaning, including the God pearl, the silence pearl, the baptism pearl, the mystery pearls and others. I've offered this bracelet as a present many times, and I still wear my own. It reminds me that there's more to life than our daily grind. It can help us to remember God and to maintain our focus on the deeper essence of life.

Sometimes we can use completely different ways to meditate – running, for instance. Through the rhythm of our movements – left, right, left, right – we can let go, and after a couple of miles the mind is free for conversation with God.

This is another area where there's no compulsion, just a wealth of possibilities from which I have to find the one that works best for me. Many of our monasteries and convents offer introductions to meditation, as well as opportunities to experience meditation as part of a group.

> Listen to your breathing
> Hear it enter –
> Hear it leave –
> And in your rhythm
> It helps you
> Have self-respect
> And come to rest
> And remain
> In this place
> Of calm
> Within you
> *Ernst Schlatter*

---

[41] See Martin Lönnebo, Carolina Welin and Carolina Johansson, *Pearls of Life: For the Personal Spiritual Journey*, Augsburg Fortress, Minneapolis, 2005.

Music

Singing has had great significance for Christianity since its birth, and through Martin Luther it became the way in which Christians of the Reformation expressed their faith. Paul Gerhardt's hymn 'O Come, My Soul, with Singing' speaks of how our whole being, from the very depths of our soul, turns to God when we sing, be it in praise or complaint, full of joy or full of care. *Nefesh*, the Hebrew word that our Bibles translate as 'soul', actually means 'throat', 'breath' or the gentle breeze that comes from the throat when one breathes out. In the Bible, this word also describes the whole person (as in Genesis 2:7) and hence means 'soul' – the living being, the seat of impulses and feelings.

It's not only our own singing, though: attending a performance or listening to a piece of music can also strengthen our faith. Some have called Johann Sebastian Bach the fifth Evangelist for the incomparable way in which his settings of the Bible transposed faith into music. 'Rejoice, exult!' from Bach's Christmas Oratorio is for me the epitome of the Christmas spirit. For many Protestants in Germany, it is the settings of Bach – and Brahms, too – that have burned Luther's translation of the Bible deep into their hearts. Bach wrote a cantata for every Sunday in the year, while Brahms's *German Requiem* explores the big questions of living and dying, death and resurrection in an utterly inimitable way.[42]

Our faith can also be given voice by quite different composers or even completely new sounds, such as the *Wasserstichorgel*, a new instrument created out of plastic tubing and buckets of water by German experimental music group the Gert Anklam Trio. Its strange tones, which can express deep calm but can also have a disturbing effect, have been used in a number of services. I'm also reminded of how a gong played a central role in the liturgy of the services at St Michael's Monastery in Hildesheim in central Germany.

---

[42] One book that contains musical settings of biblical texts is Sönke Remmert, *Bibeltexte in der Musik* (Biblical Texts in Music), Vandenhoeck and Ruprecht, Göttingen, 1996.

It's an amazing thing that, when asked to remember times when they have felt certain in their faith, many people will recount memories of singing in a choir or hearing a particular piece of music. Music is the spiritual medium *par excellence* – and that not just today. [43]

Go in search of the music that speaks to you. You might want to try to find an oratorio that you can really enter into as you hear it. Many biblical texts and other texts of our faith gain a whole new power when set to music. Some even reveal quite different meanings through their settings from those we see from simply reading them. Oratorios are performed in many churches – and not just at Christmas time. Alternatively, ask around about joining a choir. Most choirs are very happy to have new members, and they provide a way of experiencing music and community at once. Whether it's a gospel choir or a traditional choir is less important than that there be joy in song and music. Or you could simply begin to sing along with the hymns at church, to get to know the liturgy with new eyes, to hear the sounds of the organ as part of the proclamation of the Good News.

Each note arises out of the infinite silence of the earth and falls away again into the vast stillness. The elemental conversation of the silence and the music of nature gives the earth a spirit of intimacy. There is an interesting symmetry between the silence of the earth and the silence of the human body. Just as the music of the wind and water breaks the deep silence of the earth, so the sound of the word breaks the private silence of the body ... it is as though the deepest dream of silence is the beauty of music and word ... Faced with the strangeness and silence of the earth, one of the most beautiful human creations has been music. The creation of exquisite music is one of the glories of the human imagination ... Yet of course that is as we hear it. [44]

[43] Michael Nüchtern, 'Singen und Sagen: Zur Theologie der Kirchenmusik' (Singing and speaking: Towards a theology of church music) in *Glaube aktuell* (Faith Today), Evangelische Kirche in Baden, 7/3/05.

[44] John O'Donohue, *Beauty: The Invisible Embrace*, Harper Collins, New York, 2004.

Mysticism

Mysticism is perhaps the most alien approach to spirituality for us today. I found it thoroughly fascinating when Dorothee Sölle, a Protestant who had committed her life to political engagement, wrote a book in her later years on the subject of mysticism, [45] in which she gives many examples of how mysticism, this mystery, this 'longing for God', can overwhelm people and spark profound religious experiences, while at the same time wrestling to maintain the link between this mysticism and the everyday world. Even a theologian like Manfred Josuttis, who was strongly influenced by the Protestant theologian Karl Barth, has, in his most recent work, turned to the 'Saints' and become open to this strangest aspect of faith, the experiential dimension of religion. [46]

Probably the best way to approach mysticism is through its texts. [47] Anyone reading the texts can sense that they are the fruit of a deep – indeed, an overwhelming – experience of God. And yet it is the mystics themselves who are most aware, in their attempts to pin down their experiences of God in words, of the limitations of language. For this reason, mysticism is difficult to define or circumscribe. Mysticism is probably the most radical form of commitment to the path of spirituality. There are those who devote their whole lives to mysticism and encountering God. Dorothee Sölle's aim, however, is to encourage us 'to take our own experiences seriously, to save and to frame them like an important photograph'. [48] At the same time, though, I think it important to maintain a balance between keeping one's own foundations firm and being open to mystical experience, otherwise every emotional experience gets labelled a mystical one. 'If there is a Christian mysticism then such mysticism must be both inward and outward looking … Our senses should not be

[45] Dorothee Soelle, *The Silent Cry: Mysticism and Resistance*, trans. Barbara and Martin Rumscheidt, Fortress Press, Minneapolis, 2003.

[46] See Josuttis, *Heiligung des Lebens*.

[47] See, for example, Taube, *Im Innern meiner Seele ist eine Kammer*.

[48] Soelle, *The Silent Cry*, p. 15.

extinguished but rather heightened, so that we have eyes to see, and to see with amazement, and ears to hear, to hear with amazement.'[49]

Mysticism is also described as the *cognitio dei experimentalis* – the attempt to know God. The summit of this is the *unio mystica* – the union of one's soul with God, which can take the form of an experience of ecstasy. This experience requires preparation through a journey of purification and repentance, stillness and wonder. Many accounts of it speak of rapture and bliss. My belief is that this is how it feels to relinquish the world completely. At such times, it must be especially hard to keep one's biblical bearings.

As I understand it, mysticism isn't an approach to spirituality that I can take up over a weekend. I can't just try it out for a while, like taking one leg of a journey of pilgrimage. I'm not going to learn it on a course. Anyone seeking to take this journey must fundamentally rearrange their entire life; and the journey is one that can take many years. But even if we don't take this path, we can participate in it and wonder together at the remarkable writings and thoughts that the mystics have to share with us, allowing us to share something of the possibilities and profundities of encountering God.

> The unexpected presence of God would sweep over me in such a dramatic way that I could not possibly doubt that he was within me or that I was enfolded by him … In this state, the soul seems to be suspended totally outside itself. The will still loves. The memory is practically empty. And the intellect, though not completely lost, ceases to function, standing in amazement of all it suddenly understands.[50]

---

[49] *Evangelischer Erwachsenenkatechismus*, p. 246ff. (English translation prepared for this publication).

[50] Teresa of Avila, *The Book of My Life*, trans. Mirabai Starr, New Seeds Books, Boston, 2007, p. 63.

Pilgrimage

Pilgrimage, for me, is a wonderful way of combining spirituality and exercise. Many people are sceptical about pilgrimage, believing it to be just a kind of walking. Surely, they say, it's nothing more than going for a nice stroll, only with a new name that makes it look more worthy.

Where pilgrimage differs from walking is in its goals. For one thing, its literal, physical goals are different. As pilgrims, we travel down paths which Christians have walked for centuries, to reach monasteries, places of burial, and churches. Its inward goals are different, too: we go on pilgrimage because we want to deepen our faith. Experiencing nature, being aware of our bodies and talking with God or with others about faith all help towards this. To go on pilgrimage is to 'walk with God'.

The focus for today's pilgrims may not be on atonement for sins or the fulfilment of vows, as it was in the Middle Ages, but, today as ever, the desire remains to meet with God. As we travel, we are once again looking for faith. More likely than not, many who go are also hoping to put some distance between them and their everyday lives and to come closer to God through that.

One of the best-known routes of pilgrimage is the journey to Santiago de Compostela. People have been travelling this route for centuries – some to pray for the forgiveness of their sins, others to find themselves or God. I'm amazed by the effect this journey has on so many people, from famous writers to normal, everyday people.[51] Recently, Hape Kerkeling, a German comedian, joined the ranks of the pilgrims to Santiago. He's written deeply and thoughtfully about his journey, which he took 'to find God – and myself – through pilgrimage'.[52]

---

[51] See Paolo Coelho, *Diário de um mago*, Rio de Janiero, Editora Rocco, published in English as *The Pilgrimage: A Contemporary Quest for Ancient Wisdom*, trans. Alan Clarke, Harper Collins, New York, 1999.

[52] Hape Kerkeling, *Ich bin dann mal weg* (I'll Be On My Way, Then), Malik, Munich, 2006, p. 15 (English translation prepared for this publication).

The pilgrims' symbol is the scallop shell. It has its origin in a legend, but it quickly became the proof of having made the pilgrimage to Santiago. As well as being a sign of pilgrimage, it had thoroughly practical significance: it was a drinking vessel, a plate for eating and a kind of 'Swiss Army knife' for the pilgrims. Today, it has also become a symbol for pilgrims on journeys other than the Way of St James.

You may want to make a pilgrimage but not to go all the way to Spain. In Germany, you could, for instance, walk one or more stages of the new 200-mile pilgrimage route across central Germany from Volkenroda Abbey in Körner in the former East Germany, to Loccum Abbey near Hanover in the west. It was in 1163 that twelve monks from the Cistercian Abbey of Volkenroda were sent on the same journey and founded Loccum Abbey. There is a little book by Jens Gundlach that describes the various individual legs of the pilgrimage, so you can find out for yourself for how long or which section of the journey you wish to try. Along the route, many churches welcome pilgrims, offering an open church and sometimes even a bed for the night. Essentially, the pilgrimage route is constantly continuing to develop and is updated and maintained by its own users. You can read its story (in German only) at www.pilgerprojekt.de.

You can travel pilgrims' routes – this or any other – alone or with others, in silence or meditation, talking or singing. Jens Gundlach's book[53] describes the sort of experiences that are there to be had on such a pilgrimage: sacred art, the nearness of the river, people, churches, countryside, and oneself, seeing nature with new eyes and feeling one's own body letting go and finding freedom.

> Pilgrims are those who gather traces of God
> We take to the road to uncover his tracks
> with body, soul, spirit, and all the senses.
> The path leads us out to the open and, at once, into security.
> It demands a fast and promises a feast.
> Our journey can be sport or meditation,

---

[53] Jens Gundlach, *Zwischen Loccum und Volkenroda. Ein Pilgerbuch* (Between Loccum and Volkenroda: A Book of Pilgrimage), Lutherisches Verlagshaus, Hanover, 2005.

with friends or alone –
but always longing for the farther shore. [54]

Places

I love churches. Being a bishop, I get to see a huge variety of different churches just through my job – churches in villages and churches in towns, tiny chapels and vast cathedrals, Romanesque and Baroque edifices. And each of them exudes such a sense of people's love for God! True, there's sometimes a sense of self-love, too – such as when well-to-do farming villages raised grand churches just to show the world they could afford it. But often, even poor people would give their last penny, because the beauty of God needed to be visible in this place amid the often bleak realities of everyday life. Once, in Russia, I got very angry about how the people were so poor and yet the churches were so lathered with gold and grandeur, until a priest told me I needed to look at things differently. People loved to praise God in glory, he told me. It helped them to shoulder the drabness of their lives. They didn't want their church as grey as their apartments.

'See, the home of God is among mortals', says Revelation 21, describing how things will be one day, when God lives among us. Until that day, every church building is, in a sense, a temporary dwelling of God with human beings. In the heart of our villages and towns, churches keep alive the memory of the great stories of God's work among men and women. As buildings, they share the responsibility that Fulbert Steffensky ascribed to the whole Church:

> One of the fundamental political and spiritual jobs of the Church is to pass on those stories and pictures that show the value of human beings. Life is precious and loved by God; nobody should be denied their future; we are called to freedom; the first beneficiaries of the gospel are the poor – this is the message spoken, sung and played by the Judeo-Christian tradition in all its stories and images … Thus, the chief task of the Church is to proclaim

---

[54] Ibid., p. 19 (English translation prepared for this publication).

this message and paint it into people's images of life. It must remember its dreams and remember that sacrifice – this it owes to itself and to a dreamless world. [55]

When you walk inside a church you can feel that this space is special. In this place, the ancient stories are told, whose meaning reaches further than my little life and world. It is the home of the knowledge that God lives, that my life makes sense and that I am held. It is where the gospel is read – the old texts about Creation, the people of Israel, stories full of mystery and full of wisdom. They're recorded not only in words but also in pictures. And I think you can also feel that these are spaces that have been saturated in prayer. People have been bringing their joys and sorrows before God here for centuries. They've brought their children here for baptism or to consecrate themselves through communion and confirmation. They've exchanged wedding rings and held funerals for those who have died. And every Sunday, week after week, they pray: *Our Father in heaven* … That leaves its mark on a place, on a building.

In monasteries and convents, too, you can feel the spirituality of holy places. The very fact that the people who lived there dedicated their whole lives to God lends those places an atmosphere of respect for such devotion. Here, the world doesn't revolve around power, prestige and money, but around God and that which is holy. Now, obviously, monks got things wrong, too. Life in quite a few abbeys revolved around some very human, worldly concerns. Nevertheless, there remains that inkling of what is truly important – the greatness of the eternal God.

It can be a moving experience to seek and find a church, a monastery or a convent in which to pray, to keep silence, to wonder or to learn something about the faith of those who went before us. Often, the altarpieces tell the stories of the faith. They're the pictures that taught people Bible stories in

---

[55] Fulbert Steffensky, *Das Haus, das die Träume verwaltet* (The House Where Dreams Are Made), Echter, Würzburg, 2002, p. 18 (English translation prepared for this publication).

the days before they could read, or before the Bible had been transmitted in a language they could understand.

Today, education on how to 'read' churches and the symbolism within them is opening up the spirituality in these places in a completely new way. Children, young people and adults can all grasp how much love and thought went into creating them, and how much they express the faith in their aesthetics, their liturgy and their symbolism.

> These spaces invite us to participate in what they themselves are: 'the performance of the things of heaven and earth'. Entering into these spaces means entering into what they mean. If we want to understand them, we must, if only at a rudimentary level, use them in that way. Classes to experience and explore church buildings can only fulfil their potential when – without its being forced – we experience the excitement and tension of an encounter between our own individual story and the content that the space seeks to communicate. Our passion and joy, our need and desperation need to be able to be named and expressed.
>
> Church as a place of celebration, a place of lamentation and the place where we portray our vision and our utopia … Church buildings give voice to things that only they can express. There they stand, strange, amid surroundings today that crowd and besiege them. And yet this defiant strangeness is important – for the sake of our very lives.[56]

Ritual and Rhythm

Another way of bringing spirituality to life in our everyday world is by being fully conscious of living the rhythms of the year. Some rhythms are set by nature – the blossoming of spring, the days of summer and harvest time, the season of colourful leaves and the chill of winter. Most of all, though, there is the rhythm that links these seasons to Christian festivals and days of commemoration, rituals and truths.

---

[56] Roland Degen, 'Echt stark hier !' – Kirchenräume erschließen (Getting much warmer ! Making church space accessible), in Roland Degen, Inge Hansen and Christoph Scheilke (eds), *Lernort Kirchenraum: Erfahrungen – Einsichten – Anregungen* (The Church as a Place of Learning: Experiences, Insights, Ideas), Comenius-Institut, Münster, 1998, pp. 5, 18.

I would encourage you to be conscious of the church year, as you live through it. The church year begins on the first Sunday of Advent. As we light a candle, we take our first step towards the manger. Slowly, week by week, we light up the whole house. Everything has a meaning: the stars, the angels, the feast days on the way to Christmas – St Barbara, St Nicholas – and the tree. It's not just a time of fun for the children, but a time of celebration for all humanity. The Evangelical Church in Germany (EKD) has started an initiative called 'Advent is in December', which seeks to help people access the rituals and customs of Advent in a new way.[57] Advent calendars, too, can guide us wonderfully through the Advent season, thinking about what we are doing, taking a few minutes of silence each day.

Christmastide continues until Epiphany on 6 January, the day that commemorates the visit of the Magi to Jesus. Now the child's identity becomes clear – this is God's Son. After the 'ordinary time' following Epiphany comes Lent. In many parts of the world, Shrove Tuesday or Carnival is a time for great celebration, which then ends on Ash Wednesday and is succeeded by the seven weeks of Lent. Many observe this period as a special time for fasting.

Christianity's most important festival is Easter. Easter begins on Good Friday, the day of death and sorrow, and rises to the climax of that Easter morning cry of joy, 'Christ is risen! He is risen indeed, hallelujah!' Next comes Ascension Day, when we reflect on God's absence. Jesus Christ is with the Father, and yet he is not distant from us. We need to come to terms with both the nearness and the distance of God. We cannot yet follow him: we've been placed on earth to be God's witnesses in this world.

---

[57] There is a large amount of help to be found (in German) at www.advent-ist-im-dezember.de. The two calendars *Der andere Advent* (The Other Advent), which can be ordered from Andere Zeiten e.V., Heimhuderstr. 92, 20148 Hamburg or at www.anderezeiten.de) and *Advent ist im Dezember. Der Advents-Kalender* (Advent is in December – The Advent Calendar', Gütersloh), can be helpful accompaniments to the season of Advent.

At Pentecost we realize that *God is with us*! Pentecost marks the start of Trinity, a period filled with the celebrations of May, the many summer festivals and joy at God's presence. It ends with harvest thanksgiving in October, when we consciously remember all God's gifts. On that day, church altars are piled high with the fruits of the field – which also serves as an admonition to care for creation.

November is the time for mourning and remembering the dead. In Germany and in other countries, we recall those who have died in wars across the world. During November, many churches in Germany also observe Ten Days for Peace. This period comes directly before the Day of Repentance and Prayer, which Protestant churches in Germany observe on the Wednesday before the last Sunday before Advent. On this day, we bring our own sin and particularly the sins of our nation before God. The last Sunday before Advent is marked in German Protestant churches as Eternity Sunday, as an opportunity to remember those who have died during the year. In many parishes, the names of those who have passed on are read out individually, and we take comfort from God's words in the Bible, when he says, 'I have called you by name; you are mine' (Isaiah 43:1).

This is only a snapshot of all the rites that exist. I always think that they are in wonderful harmony with the rhythms of nature. To observe those rhythms – to be able to wait and not start putting out Christmas trees and Santas in mid-August – is healthy, both for one's own soul and for a society. For if we have everything all at once, in reality we have nothing anymore. We end up with a kind of collective burn-out.

You can organize your own year by these rites. You will discover many of them for the first time – and so may your whole family. In addition, there are also certain times dedicated to specific people: in Germany in 2006, for instance, we remembered the birth of Dietrich Bonhoeffer, while in 2007 we commemorated that of Elizabeth of Thuringia. At the very least, it's healthy to give one's life rhythm, to recognize special seasons, to prepare oneself and have patience, to experience the events in our lives with pleasure and fasting, anticipation and waiting. This area of spirituality is most especially for every day. It gives us seasons that we can experience, guided through them by the Bible and tradition.

> The day thou gavest, Lord, is ended,
> the darkness falls at thy behest;
> to thee our morning hymns ascended,
> thy praise shall sanctify our rest.
>
> As o'er each continent and island
> the dawn leads on another day,
> the voice of prayer is never silent,
> nor dies the strain of praise away.
>
> The sun that bids us rest is waking
> our friends beneath the western sky,
> and hour by hour fresh lips are making
> thy wondrous doings heard on high.
>
> So be it, Lord; thy throne shall never,
> like earth's proud empires, pass away:
> thy kingdom stands, and grows forever,
> till all Thy creatures own thy sway.
> *John Ellerton* [58]

Saints

Many people today have a hard time knowing how to deal with the veneration of saints. Some say, 'It's nothing but stories', while others believe the saints are examples in faith. Still others say that this practice leads our faith astray, while another group thinks it incredibly important to remember the martyr whose name they bear on their name day, for instance, or to have that saint as the patron of their own church.

A while ago I celebrated an anniversary service at a Lutheran convent in Germany. The service is held every year on St Bartholomew's Day, 24 August, for it was on that date that the convent was first consecrated, and on the same date that the rebuilt convent was consecrated, at a new site,

---

[58] In *Rejoice and Sing* (full music edition), Oxford University Press, Oxford, 1991, p. 835.

around 200 years ago following a fire. Bartholomew and his story therefore mean a lot to this (Protestant!) community. As the procession entered the church, it carried a large figure into the sanctuary – I was told it was St Maurice. The figure has black skin – a positively anti-racist symbol in this day and age. I only read his story afterwards, in an encyclopedia.[59] The two saints, as witnesses to the faith, clearly forged a link to this place that still binds people to their memory down the centuries.

Many of the legends concerning the saints have been wildly embellished and are hardly comprehensible to us today. The stories of who spilled what blood where in which martyrdom can sometimes be positively gory, and I don't find they strengthen my faith especially well. And yet there is a very important idea behind them: we are remembering those who have believed before us. We maintain a culture of remembrance, a memory. Now obviously, in Protestantism, this isn't going to turn into the veneration of the saints. But to think of those who have gone before us, who stood up for their faith in difficult times – that means something to us, too. Indeed, in this there may well be something of ecumenical value to be discovered.[60]

Nevertheless, Protestants will always instinctively stress that making someone a saint has nothing to do with putting human beings on a pedestal. Instead, it means honouring those who have completely and utterly devoted their lives to God. Time and again, the relationships between denominations have faced challenges with regard to calling someone a saint or blessed. Indeed, even on the Roman Catholic side of the fence, the issue has been formulated thus: 'Perhaps the most convincing form of ecumenism is the ecumenism of the saints and of the martyrs. The

---

[59] See, for example, 'Maurice and Companions' in the *Oxford Dictionary of Saints*, 4th edn., ed. D. H. Farmer, Oxford University Press, Oxford, 1997, p. 341.

[60] See Walter Fleischmann-Bisten, 'Vorbilder im Glauben oder "schwierige heilige"?' (Examples in faith or 'difficult saints'?) in *Materialdienst des Konfessionskundlichen Instituts Bensheim*, 04/2006, p. 71f.

communio sanctorum speaks louder than the things which divide us.'[61]

Perhaps through this approach we will be able to reach common ground. The process was recently given an exciting new momentum with the publication of a book on Protestant martyrs of the twentieth century.[62] It has nothing to do with praying to certain individuals. It has to do with remembering our sisters and brothers in the faith who have had the courage to stand up for their beliefs. 'Remember!' and 'Do not forget!' are constant challenges throughout the Bible: the memories of Adam and Eve, Abraham and Sarah, Isaac and Rebekah are ones that give us bearings to follow and weave a web of stories in which we can have our own thread. Memory of this kind has a spiritual dimension, as it strengthens us in our own faith, and an ecumenical dimension, because it relates to our common ancestors in the faith.

And so I'd like to encourage you to find your own 'saint', not as some kind of mediator between you and God (of course!), but as a person from history who truly lived his or her faith. I think we have a deal to learn from our fathers and mothers in the faith. And I think, when we immerse ourselves in the history of Christianity, we can draw strength from the way others confronted far harder challenges than we face and how God gave them the strength not to despair but to stand firm. To see that can shore up our trust in God, when we are tempted to despair of our own weak faith or fear that it's not strong or true enough.

Have a look to see if you have a namesake in the Canon of Saints. Alternatively, it may be that your birthday falls on a day of special commemoration. Or you might discover a father or mother in the faith who makes a particular impression on you or moves you or makes you stop and think. We

---

[61] Apostolic Visit of His Holiness Pope John Paul II to Azerbaijan and Bulgaria, Homily of the Holy Father, Plovdiv, Sunday 26 May 2002.

[62] H. Schultze and A. Kurschat (eds), *'Ihr Ende schaut an ...' Evangelische Märtyrer des 20. Jahrhunderts* ('Consider the Outcome of Their Way of Life': Protestant Martyrs of the Twentieth Century), Evangelische Verlagsanstalt, Leipzig, 2006.

can learn much for our own life of faith from the memory and commemoration of other people's stories.

> Of the Worship of Saints they teach that the memory of saints may be set before us, to strengthen our faith when we see the grace they were given and the way in which they were helped through faith; also that we may follow their faith and good works, according to our calling ... But the Scripture teaches not the invocation of saints or to ask help of saints, since it sets before us the one Christ as the Mediator, Propitiation, High Priest, and Intercessor (1 Timothy 2:5). (Augsburg Confession, Article XXI)

Stillness

We seldom hear silence in our world today. Noise marks every aspect of our days. Traffic, radio, television and telephones are everywhere. Noise upon noise positively besieges us: music plays in the background as we shop; market traders shout above the traffic; the TV competes to be heard above the vacuum cleaner; the radio prattles away as we work.

Many seek silence in nature. And it's there to be found, even today. I recently went on a cycling tour of the River Elbe and, on stopping for a break, suddenly became aware of perfect quiet, broken only by a breath of wind or a chirruping bird. That was the first time I'd noticed just what a rare thing silence is. Times like that remind me of Elijah's experience, hiding in the crevice in the mountainside. It's written that God showed him his presence as he passed by, but not in a storm, nor an earthquake, nor a fire, but in a still, small whisper (1 Kings 19:12). Yes, even while many seek the divine in that which is powerful and strong, in powerful thunder and loud cataracts, God is to be found in stillness and gentleness.

When we create space for silence, we are enabling an experience of God. There are no distractions. But we can't just jump into silence as if it were a swimming pool. We must find our way into silence slowly, through much practice. Quietness is impossible unless we ourselves are quiet. And yet, alongside this, it also requires others to be quiet as well. Silence is something that has to be observed either by agreement with others or in a special place of quiet. This place has to be somewhere where one can distance oneself from all the noises of everyday life. There's no point looking for silence in the middle of Hanover or Munich or on the heaving, crowded beaches of Majorca. There's silence in nature. There can be silence in churches. But nowhere is better suited to finding silence than a monastery or convent. These monastic spaces were made for silence – they just breathe stillness. I've noticed even tourists, just sightseeing around a monastery or convent, will lower their voices and become quieter because they can feel it: this is a place of quiet. You can experience that in churches as well. Just the feeling of certain spaces can inspire us to meditation.

The Bible tells us that Jesus himself went into the wilderness to seek clarity about his own mission. It also tells how he would leave his disciples and climb up onto a mountain or keep watch in the garden of Gethsemane to talk with God. Creating distance from the everyday and sometimes spending time away from those we love can be important in helpings us to straighten ourselves out, distinguish between what's important and what's not and provide some space for God and for our faith.

Many people who deliberately seek spiritual experiences through silence find that they do come, but slowly, step by step. Quietness can be too intense, can make us anxious. For that reason, it's good to allow others to guide us into stillness – and back out again! Alternatively, we can find our own point of entry, feeling our way in. Nobody should try to force long periods of silence on themselves all at once. This can feel anxious or oppressive; it can make one feel alone or frightened. Nevertheless, the search for greater depth in our faith can be helped by building in periods of quiet during each day or each week. Just as with being silent ourselves, the important thing is to find our own way in, our own rhythm, our own ways and times for experiencing stillness.

Silence

All that is great
Comes from silence.
Those who were great
Have sought silence.
They were shaped
In the wilderness:
Moses, Jesus, Paul.
Monks gathered silence
Into their cloisters.
And their writing,
Their chanting, their working
Live on.
In silence a person forms
Inside a mother's body.
In silence people
Find each other.
In silence the infinite
Mystery,
The deep You,
Draws people on.
In the silence of the night
Jacob wrestled with God. [63]

---

[63] Martin Gutl, 'In der Stille', *Nachdenken mit Martin Gutl. Texte Meditationen, Gebete* (Reflections with Martin Gutl: Texts, Meditations, Prayers), Styria, Graz, 1983 (English translation prepared for this publication).

Afterword

This book outlines a sort of short exploration of some specific questions. How can we approach spirituality? Where can we be sure of the ground beneath our feet? What are the tensions that we need to be aware of? What opportunities can we try to take?

At the same time as I was writing this text, I was asking my own personal questions. I was ill in mid- and late 2006, and my illness gave me an opportunity and a need to think very deliberately about where to find support that would uphold me at a time when life's big questions stopped being theoretical and became reality in my own life. As I read, reflected and wrote, it confirmed my belief that we can find support in tradition, in the Bible, prayer, worship and in our heritage of hymns and song, as set out in the first part of this book.

There are many other possibilities, and I'd always support the people of our church in looking for their own paths and opening new doors. But the capacity to trust in God does not just fall out of the sky like that. And when our own words fail, we need to rely on the words of those who have lived their faith out before us, or on an old melody that was comforting people long before we were even born.

I was recently at a public debate in Leipzig where a young man rounded on me and said, 'All your ancient texts and your old-fashioned songs and your stuffy services – what can they possibly say to me?' Here was someone who was 27 years old, clearly searching for faith, or he would never have come to an event with a bishop, and I think we need to offer him something. At the same time, though, we can't trim everything down into media-friendly, bite-sized chunks. Faith takes time, commitment – a quest. Someone once said, 'Church is fitness training for the soul.' It's an incomplete, sloppy little soundbite, but it makes an important point. People will spend a lot of time and, indeed, money going to the gym, and yet our soul needs this time as well. You can't simply switch faith on like an electric light. It grows with us through our lives, through our experiences with God, and also through our darkest days, our tears and desperation. We need to make space for our souls and time for our faith.